Giving:

God's Heart

In You

Jim Inkster

Published by 5 Smooth Stones

5 SMOOTH STONES

Kelowna, BC
Canada

ISBN-13: 978-1-9994251-0-4

DEDICATION

To my lovely wife, Bonnie, who always says yes every time I ask if we should give.

CONTENTS

ACKNOWLEDGMENTS

I would like to thank my lovely wife, Bonnie, who not only gave me feedback on the manuscript but lived and experienced this life journey of faith with me. I would like to thank the Lord whose Holy Spirit breathed revelation on His Holy Scriptures and opened the eyes of my understanding to the true nature of my Father in Heaven.

1 In the Beginning

As a child I was very close to any money I received. My favourite Christmas gift always came from an uncle who would give me a brand new freshly minted one-dollar coin in a case. Oooh, I loved those shiny coins! I would stash it away with my other coins and currency. One of the biggest tragedies in my young life was losing my wallet whilst on an errand to the grocery store for my mother. My older brother and I scoured the route I had taken to the store and then went to the police station to report it missing with the hope someone had turned it in. I lost all of five dollars and a beautiful golden brown leather wallet.

My father used to tease me about having the first dollar I ever received. At other times he would say I was so tight with money that I squeaked when I walked. In primary – elementary school every year our teacher would ask what we wanted to be when we grew up. Many said firemen, pilots and policemen but I always said I was going to be a millionaire. Everyone wanted to know what I would do to earn this to which I shrugged my shoulders and said I didn't know. It seemed impossible in those days to earn such a huge amount of money but I wasn't fazed. I knew I loved money.

The problem with loving money is it controlled me.

The problem with loving money is it controlled me. I couldn't give it away no matter how noble and right the cause might be. I couldn't run a budget either as I would scrimp even more. I remember needing a light bulb for a study lamp. I stood in the store contemplating the cost of each one until I finally left empty-handed as I thought I could move my desk over by the window and work with that diminished light.

I didn't realize how other people saw me. I just had a value that majorly shaped my decisions. Even if I had earned millions I would have had a tough time enjoying them. As I said money owned me, not the other way round.

Then I became a Christian, a follower of Jesus. I came to a revelation of who He was through reading the bible and praying. One evening while my wife was at a church meeting I was about to spend the time alone looking at some unsavoury material. But I thought I should read my bible first. I was in a hurry so I cut the bible open at Revelation 3. My eyes fell upon verses 15 and 16. "I know all the things you do, that you are neither hot nor cold. I wish that you were one or the other! But since you are like lukewarm water, neither hot nor cold, I will spit you out of my mouth!" The paraphrased version I was reading then said I will vomit you out of my mouth. I was so shocked for it was as if Jesus was standing next to the bed speaking to me. I was instantly convicted; as I would run hot at meetings we had attended only to wake the next morning saying, I don't think I really believe in Jesus. Hot and cold! I said out loud 'what do I do, Lord?' I looked back down at verse 20, which said: "Look! I stand at the door and knock. If you hear my voice and open the door, I will come in, and we will share a meal together as friends." I knelt at the side of my bed and asked Him to come into my life and share His life intimately with me. I proclaimed my commitment to Him when my wife came home and at every meeting for a month after that.

I knew I was a new creation. The hunger I had for His word increased even more from that point on. One matter that intrigued my wife and I is the issue of giving. We read about the tithe and giving throughout the word. Here was the man who squeaked when he walked wanting to know how to give to God. I freely and willingly wanted to give and to understand how to do it right. It changed my life from being wholly surrendered to the almighty dollar to surrendering the almighty dollar to my new Lord and King.

As I have contemplated the material that I would write about I have come to realize that a book on giving is really writing about the Father's heart. How can that be, you may ask? Hopefully the following vignette I imagined will help you envision the giving of our Heavenly Lord.

* * *

The expanse was quiet as they sat opposite each other in silent contemplation. No one said anything, only silence. Their faces were unmoved, not a muscle twitch or a blink of the eyelid to indicate any emotion. The silence seemed to last an eternity. Finally, a word was spoken.

"That settles it then."

"Do we have any other choice?" (A rhetorical question, for every option had been exhaustively pursued.)

"If we want them to be truly free and true to us, then this is the only course of action."

"Are we in agreement? We have to be, for it will cost us all immensely."

"Well, before we settle this, I have one question. Is there no doubt that they will make the wrong choice? Don't answer that, I know what they will do."

"Well, it will be good, only very, very costly."

Arising and clasping hands they smiled. In unison they said: "Let's do it. Let's make man in our image."

The word was spoken, the man formed from the dust, and the Father breathed His Spirit into the man's mouth and he became a living soul.

*   *   *

Impossible! I don't think so. The bible tells us that Jesus was the lamb slain from the foundation of the world. The decision to give His life to pay the price for our sin was made before we were formed. God the Father, God the Son, and God the Holy Spirit knew the cost of fellowship with man was expensive, yet they chose to create man all the same.

Let me personalize John 3:16 for us. "God so loved you and I that He sent His son so that you and I may live and have eternal life if we chose to believe in Him." We have to grasp that the decision to give so extravagantly was made even though they knew that Adam would sin by disobeying the command to not eat the fruit from the tree of the knowledge of good and evil.

How can that be?

Such incredible extravagance!

The Father's heart was and is to give everything for us. He did it while we were not worthy and full of disobedience. He gave us love so that we could love Him. He has constantly and consistently given to mankind. He created the earth and everything on, in and above it, and then, gave it to man to rule over and to care for it. He has given to us the glorious opportunity to have fellowship with Him restored through the sacrifice of Jesus. He has given us time to repent. He is long-suffering and not quick to judge. He is constantly giving and giving to mankind.

If we don't understand giving, we don't understand God. When we accept the gift of life through believing on Christ, we are given His life. I exchange my life for His. My old nature is dead. His nature now lives in me. In fact the word says that He gave us the gift of faith through which we believe unto our salvation. We didn't need to manufacture faith or depend on something we worked up to believe. He gave us the gift of faith to believe.

Giving throbs through our bodies, as does the Holy Spirit.

If we do not feel moved to give and to bless, we might ask ourselves: "Are we truly born again?" If we fight the urge to respond to the needs of others or to offerings, are we not really fighting our own new nature? The voice saying: "Give" is not the Devil. It is the Holy Spirit within us who is transforming us into the image of Jesus. As believers our very nature is to give. We actually gave our life away at the time we received Christ. Through water baptism we laid down our life to receive His life. This is who we are. We are givers. Giving throbs through our bodies, as does the Holy Spirit.

It is time to embrace the Father's heart for our lives. It is time to manifest the true nature of Christ living in us. It is time to give freely without obligation or under compulsion. It is time for us to be all that God intended us to be – in the image of Him.

The chapters that follow begin with a vignette that could occur in a believer's life. It is hoped it will help the reader identify the prompting of the Holy Spirit in their life. Following each vignette there is teaching that brings the grace and truth of God's word to life for the reader. There is one chapter where questions are substituted for the vignette.

May you read on and enjoy God's wonderful gift of giving to you. My prayer is that these chapters will bring you revelation of the height, depth, width and length of the Lord's love for you as well as answering questions that needed an answer before you could give freely and cheerfully.

2 Treasure of the Heart

'Oh, this is all I need. What happened to that late day rally?'

As Ivan paced his office his composure was quickly slipping away. He struggled to loosen his tie, to get some breath. It all seemed surreal. He changed the channel on one of the three monitors that were blaring a cacophony of figures, percentages and spiraling indexes. Maybe the sports network would get his mind off of it. His thoughts were not abating with the seemingly endless volleying of the tennis ball. He felt like a fox terrified by the baying of the hounds.

Where could he run? Where could he hide? There's no escaping. I'm trapped... trapped... trapped!

His chest burned. Was it that stomach condition he had developed from the greasy takeaways he'd eaten in the office?

He caught his image in the mirror behind his desk. God, what happened? You used to be so trim. Irene was right; I should have used that gym membership I purchased. Man, I look like a designer suit full of overstuffed pillows.

What did that financial reporter say? The pain seared through his temple. Where are those painkilling tablets? Whatever you do, don't look at the price quotes on the other monitor. Noooo, they've dropped again! Close the market, close the market, please close the market...

Ow, that pain! Oh man, my arms feel numb and weird! Where are those pills? Blast, I broke the glass in Irene's favourite photo of our house. Wish I had spent more time there than here. Then maybe I wouldn't have made that investment.

Gasping for air he collapsed into his executive leather chair. God, its killing me was his last thought.

* * *

"For where your treasure is, there your heart will be also."

Giving is a heart issue.

Where is your treasure? Is it in all the promises of God? Is it in celebration and dance? Is it in prophecy and moving in words of knowledge? Where is your heart?

Giving is a heart issue. It reveals what we really

believe. If we can give, we believe God and His word that says to seek first the kingdom of God and His righteousness and all these other things will be added unto you. God doesn't say give and you won't have. He promises that what we give will be multiplied back to us. It is like seed. A seed planted will produce many more seeds - seeds for food and seeds for planting. It is a kingdom principle woven into the very fabric of the earth.

Why do we ignore this principle if it is found in nature and in God's word? It's because of our heart. Our heart is where our treasure is. If our treasure is here on earth, it is very hard to respond to a heavenly request.

When a rich young man approached Jesus, he wanted to have eternal life. He desired to go to heaven. Jesus told him to obey the Ten Commandments. The young man told him that he had kept them since he was a child. Jesus, we are told, loved him and He touched his heart with His words. He told him to sell all that he had and give it to the poor. The young man couldn't do it for he was wealthy. What a price Jesus was asking of him? He was wealthy and young. Obviously he was a mover and shaker in the world of commerce. He had it all. But Jesus told him that to give it all away was the key to eternal life for him. Why?

Where was his heart? It was with his treasure.

Peter, having observed this exchange, said to Jesus: "What's in it for us, since we have left everything?" Jesus gave us a wonderful promise in response to Peter's question. "I tell you the truth, no one who has left home or brothers or sisters or mother or father or children or fields for me and the gospel will fail to receive a hundred times as much in this present age (homes, brothers, sisters, mothers, children and fields - and with them, persecutions) and in the age to come, eternal life." Mark 10:29, 30

The problem for Peter and the boys was they actually hadn't left everything. Peter, even after seeing the resurrected Christ, led a number of the twelve off to go fishing. What? How could Peter do that? Didn't he say that they had left everything?

Yes, he was disheartened. Yes, he needed to be reinstated by Jesus. But, the point is, he still had his boat, net and all the equipment. He had his safety net to fall back on at the time he questioned Jesus. What's in it for me? What's the treasure?

> *Where is our treasure?*

Where your treasure is, there is your heart. Why do you think in 2 Corinthians 9 God says through Paul don't give grudgingly or under compulsion? Because it is a heart issue! He wants you to invest only where your heart is. God is interested in our heart condition.

He chose David as King because he was a man after God's heart. He wanted what God wanted. He was only interested in pleasing God. When he was wrong, he was quick to repent because he did not want to be out of heart relationship with his Lord. The Lord is looking for those whose hearts are after his. Giving let's us see where we have set our heart. It lets us know what God already knows about us. If we struggle in this area, we need to turn to Him and seek where we need to change our minds so that we have our heart in the right place.

Where is our treasure?

3 Reflecting Our Nature

Nigel and Sue sat in silence in the luxury of their five star hotel room, both feeling an increasing discomfort as the weekend progressed. Neither could initially tell what was making them uneasy. It seemed very unusual to feel like this, as it was a holiday that they had looked forward to for some time. Tim and Naomi, friends of some financial means, had asked them to come with them to the city as their guests. They had planned the holiday including the evening at the theatre with all expenses paid. What was to be a blessing was now feeling very uncomfortable.

Sue broke the silence with a sigh. "Why do I feel so unhappy?"

"Uh?" groaned Nigel, shaken from deep thought.

"Why do I feel so unhappy, so uncomfortable this weekend?" Sue reiterated.

"Strange, so do I. I have been trying to understand why I feel like a kept man," said Nigel. "It seems as if I am being tied up with ropes, with no freedom to move. I feel like I have to ask for everything and that I meet with huge disapproval when I do."

"That's exactly it", replied Sue. "I felt that Tim and Naomi were very generous with their money and wanted to bless us with a break that we so desperately needed. Instead I feel from them this reluctance to give even though they do. It makes me feel very uncomfortable and it's hard to relax, which is what this holiday was supposed to be about."

"I agree. It reminds me of that proverb that says, 'Do not eat the food of a stingy man; do not crave his delicacies; for he is the kind of man who is always thinking about the cost. "Eat and drink," he says to you, but his heart is not with you. You will vomit up the little you have eaten and will have wasted your compliments.' I may not vomit but I do feel tight in the stomach and generally uneasy."

"I know what you mean. Well, only twelve more hours and we'll be home."

*   *   *

What's the problem? Well, it's a heart issue. People can't truly hide what is in their heart. That's why we can see in 2 Corinthians 9:7 that each man should give what he has decided in his heart to give, not reluctantly or under compulsion, for God loves a cheerful giver. It is a heart issue. God is not putting anyone under compulsion to do anything. In fact in

People can't truly hide what is in their heart.

Proverbs he warns against partaking of hospitality offered by a man with a wrong heart attitude. People are adept at communicating without words. If a person is not happy about giving, then others will know about it whether they say something or not. Giving reflects on their heart attitude that reveals their attitude to God.

Prior to being born again in which you receive a new soft heart sin encrusts our heart to the point that it becomes like stone. We become unmoved by the needs and problems of others. Our old nature builds walls behind which to hide and to live a life of self-preservation. In some cases this is done in the natural with people moving onto land away from neighbours and community. Isolation is considered protection from the encroachment of people and their problems.

When we receive Christ, we become new creatures with new hearts. In fact the bible tells us that He takes up residence in our heart through the Holy Spirit. Colossians says that all the fullness of the godhead dwells in Christ and He dwells in us. When we partake in baptism, we are recognizing our death and His resurrection in our life. It is no longer I that lives but He in me. In other words his nature is downloaded into us.

We now have a nature that is loving, compassionate, merciful and giving. As Jesus was moved by compassion so to will we be. That prompting that we feel to pray for the sick, the lame and the paralyzed is not from our old nature. We would have avoided those people before if we could. That prompting is the Holy Spirit in you stirring you to be Christ to someone else.

> *We now have a nature that is loving, compassionate, merciful and giving.*

When Jesus was on earth, he trained his disciples to do what he was doing. He told them to wait for the power of the Holy Spirit to come upon them and that they were to be his witnesses to his resurrection with power. We are to share the word of a risen saviour and watch as the Holy Spirit confirms with signs and wonders following. That is God's plan for us. That is the work of the Holy Spirit within us. We are not the author of these thoughts nor is it the

Devil. We are feeling the throbbing of our new heart; one full of compassion and giving.

God gave Adam dominion over the earth. He gave Abraham a son of promise. He gave the sons of Israel the blood of the lamb to cover them from his judgement of Egypt. He gave Israel the land of Canaan. He gave mankind His son who takes away the sins of the world. Jesus gave away his position within the godhead to become a man and to identify with us in our fallen humanity. He willing laid down his life as an atoning sacrifice for us so that by believing on Him we can have eternal life. He went to the Father on our behalf with His blood as an acceptable sacrifice once and for all. Jesus sent us His Holy Spirit so we would have a comforter, counsellor and teacher.

It is God's very nature to give.

It is God's very nature to give. It was this very issue that Satan chose to try to deceive Eve with. He accused God of withholding something from them. It is Satan's nature to withhold and hoard and covet but it is not God's.

Romans 6 tell us that in receiving Christ and identifying with Him in His death we are no longer slaves to sin and our old nature. Paul exhorts us to no longer walk in the old nature but to walk in the Spirit. He tells us to be renewed in our thinking and to no longer continue in the futility of our old ways. There is a point of application for us. It is to respond to that prompting to give rather than withhold.

If you have become a believer in Christ and have yielded your life to Him, then you will find that the Lord is working his nature into your life. You will be conformed to the image of His son, Jesus. He will not leave his children in the squalor of darkness. His Holy Spirit will stir and stir within you to change your mind and your ways. It is unwise to resist the work of God in our life. He took you at your word when you surrendered to Him. He will not go away and give up. You can try and ignore Him but He won't go away. There is a battle raging to have you deny who you truly are.

When you get those prompting to give, do it. Follow the tug of your heart. Give willingly and without compulsion. He won't prompt you to do something that He won't give you the ability to perform.

4 A Commanding Promise

Josh was alone in the office, only the desk light in his cubicle illuminating the darkness. His computer screen flickered as he stared at his latest creation. He leaned back in his swivel chair thinking of how worthwhile it was to stay late. In the silence you could really think and let the creative juices flow.

He was startled when a hand suddenly touched his shoulder. Swinging around in fear and anticipation of the worst he was even more startled by what he saw.

Standing before him was a bearded man in a business suit and dress shoes. There was a radiant glow about his whole body. Josh was stunned, his mouth hung open with the slackness of utter surprise.

Before he could speak the man asked him a question. "Do you know who I am?" Josh's initial response was "no" but before he could utter a word he had a strange impression that this was Jesus. The man smiled and said, "What's the matter, the cat got your tongue?"

Josh cleared his throat and said, "Jesus?"

"Ah, revelation?" responded the man. "Do you love me?"

"Of.... of.... of course I do," replied Josh.

"Do you love me?"

Josh thought why on earth is he asking me again. I have gone to Sunday school, gone forward in church to receive him into my life at least three times that I can remember clearly. Yeah, I love him. "I love you," he said.

"Do you love me?"

His eyes seem to be looking right into my soul thought Josh. An ache welled up within him. "I love you," he said emphatically.

"Then do what I have commanded."

"What?"

He vanished.

* * *

Jesus says that we are truly his disciples if we love him and obey all that he commanded us to do. In John 14:21 Jesus states: "Whoever has my commands and obeys them, he is the one who loves me. He who loves me will be loved by my Father, and I too will love him and show myself to him." What does he mean? If we are saved by grace and not by good works that we have done ourselves, are we supposed to work and obey commands to earn and retain our salvation? No! The fact is - he has done the work. There is nothing we can add to make it more complete, or do that will be of credit to us. But if we are saved, that is we truly believe in Him, then we are a new creation in Christ. If we love Him and have his life in us, we will reflect who He is to the world around us. We would obviously obey the one we love and have yielded our life to. This is an outward sign of our inward submission to Him. We would do the things that He has commanded and we wouldn't find them a burden.

We will reflect who He is to the world around us.

For example, on a natural plane, I love my wife dearly. Because I do, I do not find it a burden to bless her when she asks me to get her something. Sometimes it is not convenient, and sometimes I feel lazy and do not want to move, but the pleasure it brings her when I respond blesses me. She feels valued and loved and responds to me even more lovingly than before. If we love Him, then we will respond to His commands. It may not be convenient or expedient or seem the wisest thing at the time, but it blesses Him when we respond in obedience and out of love. We do not have the advantage of a heavenly perspective to see what that act of obedience will release. We may think that we can't afford to give or to stop and pray for someone due to what appears to be very responsible reasons. We may think it just isn't prudent to give that money because we have rent due or need some food or were planning to go out to dinner with it. But we can't see what God has planned for us; the only way to find out is to respond with obedience to the prompting of the Holy Spirit.

What then has He commanded us to do? He has commanded us to forgive as we have been forgiven. He has asked us to let our words be true and to speak in love to one another. He has asked us to honour our father and mother, the command with a promise. He said if we did, things will go well for us and we will have a long life. Another significant command of His is to give. In Luke 6:38 Jesus says: "Give, and it will be given to you. A good measure, pressed down, shaken together and running over, will be poured into your lap. For with the measure you use, it will be measured to you." It is a command with a promise attached to it. He says that what we receive is tied directly to what we give. If we are abundant in our giving, we will receive abundantly. If we are sparse in our giving, we will find ourselves recipients of sparseness in our own lives.

We can trust that what He says is what He means.

God says in His word that He is not a man that he should lie. We can trust that what He says is what He means. We believe it for our salvation. I have complete confidence in His word that tells me that by believing in Christ I will go to heaven. My eternal salvation is secure in my mind because I believe that what He said is true. Well, what about the rest of the things He has told us to do? Do we debate them or do we honour them because they are true? He said that we would receive by a good measure, pressed down, shaken together and running over. This was an illustration of a familiar image during His time on earth. When they bought grain in the market, it was measured out into the folds of the purchaser's robes as they held them out. Jesus says that the amount given to you will be poured in, shaken down to get more in, and then will overflow the edges. It will be in abundance.

5 The Return on Investment

"Hey Jess, look what I found in the mailbox."

"What's so interesting, Tim?"

"No stamp, no address, just my name on the envelope."

"Well, open it. This is so exciting!"

"Wow, a thousand dollars in crisp new hundred dollar bills. Praise God!"

"A thousand dollars?"

"Yeah."

"Whose it from?"

"No name, just money, exactly what I had been praying and hoping for. Yahoo!"

"Humph! Why does that always happen to you? I give a tithe from my salary like you. Why do you keep getting blessed with finances and I don't?"

"I'm sorry, Jess, I didn't know it was there and that it would upset you."

"It does and it doesn't. I mean", Jess said as she snatched some of the bills, "what's yours is mine, but why don't I get blessed like you?"

"Well – maybe it has to do with how you view tithing and your expectancy."

"What do you mean?"

"I mean, do you see tithing as sort of a God tax or penalty, almost like government taxes? Or do you see it as an investment where you expect a return?"

"I see it as something God expects from me. It's better to give than to receive, you know. So I don't give to get. I would never do that, I mean, expect a return."

"There's your reason."

* * *

I think that many believers do see the tithe as an additional tax that's being levied against their income. They struggle with it because the government is already taking a share of it, which grows in percentage of how much they take as you earn more. Rarely do the taxpayers become the direct beneficiaries of the government taxation. If we pay taxes we don't expect them to give exponential amounts back to us. If we gave them $1000.00 we would not expect $10,000.00 or $100,000.00 coming back to us. They simply take and take and take some more.

And yet many believers struggle with the concept that there is a return promised by God in response to their giving. They feel it is wrong to give with an expectation of receiving a return on the money. Some how they feel it is less godly to give with an expectancy of financial reward. Yet the bible says: "Give, and it will be given to you. A good measure, pressed down, shaken together and running over, will be poured into your lap. For with the measure you use, it will be measured to you." (Luke 6:38) It is quite clear in this verse that giving will be rewarded as a reciprocal response to the gift. Not only that, it will overflow to you. This is a picture of purchasing grain in the market. The purchaser would hold up the hem of their robe, forming a bowl into which the vendor poured out the measure of grain. Jesus says that it will be returned to you overflowing your garment's capacity. Even with being pressed down and shaken together it will overflow. A caveat to receiving this amount of return is the qualification that your giving determines your receiving. What measure do you use? Do you give a lot or a bit? That measure affects your return. Everyone I know or have heard of who determined to give more that 10% are overwhelmed by how much comes back to them.

Yet, believers struggle with this concept. Many people in the church have told me that they would never give to get more money back. It sounds very noble but it isn't scriptural. I know I have thought that way at one time. For me it was the concern that I am getting benefit from something that should be charitable, i.e., to dispense assistance to the needy. Is my motive right in helping them if I'm expecting a return? Am I just doing this to get more money to spend upon myself?

But – God clearly says in Deuteronomy 8:17

and 18, "You may say to yourself, "My power and the strength of my hands have produced this wealth for me." But remember the LORD your God, for it is he who gives you the ability to produce wealth, and so confirms his covenant, which he swore to your ancestors, as it is today." He gives us the ability to produce wealth. In fact it is a confirmation of His covenant with us. That ability may create wealth through what we do with our hands but it will also come to us through our generosity to others.

God is going to reward your giving.

Paul writes to the Corinthians in his second letter and the ninth chapter about their giving. He says "and God is able to bless you abundantly, so that in all things at all times, having all that you need, you will abound in every good work. As it is written: "They have freely scattered their gifts to the poor; their righteousness endures forever." Now he who supplies seed to the sower and bread for food will also supply and increase your store of seed and will enlarge the harvest of your righteousness. You will be enriched in every way so that you can be generous on every occasion, and through us your generosity will result in thanksgiving to God." It is clear that God is going to reward your giving. As a farmer sows seed upon his fields he expects a harvest that will replace his initial outlay of seed and provide an abundance to produce bread for sale. Similarly God is saying He will supply the seed you are sowing and enlarge your harvest of righteousness. You will be enriched, i.e., that is make you wealthier, so you can be generous. This is not about hoarding for your future. It is talking about a dynamic life of giving and receiving, which amazingly leads to righteousness.

Righteousness is simply doing what is right in God's eyes. He says in verse 12 of the chapter that "this service that you perform is not only supplying the needs of the Lord's people but is also overflowing in many expressions of thanks to God". When we give to people they respond with thankfulness to God, which blesses Him. Then they bless you for verse 14 says 'in their prayers for you their hearts will go out to you, because of the surpassing grace God has given you'.

In chapter 8 of 2 Corinthians Paul is talking about the Macedonian believers and their desire to give, which excelled any expectations he had of how generous they would be. Verses 6 and 7 say "So we urged Titus, just as he had earlier made a beginning, to bring also to completion **this act of grace** on your part. But since you excel in everything—in faith, in speech, in knowledge, in complete earnestness and in the love we have kindled in you —see that you also **excel in this grace of giving"**. This is neither a law to be fulfilled nor a tax to be paid. It is all an action of grace that divine influence upon the heart and its outward working. Grace, grace, grace of giving!

We received this grace when we first were saved from this present darkness, the rule of the prince of the power of the air. We were delivered into Jesus' incredible light and presence. We have huge expectations of resurrection from the dead, a glorious immortal body and to dwell in His presence and glory for eternity. We expect all this through the grace that was given to us. We can also expect that well we are on this earth in this present age that if we give, He will multiply it back to us so that we can give again and again as representatives of His righteous nature.

It is not a tax. It is not a penalty. It will not

lead to poverty.

It is His word. It is His promise. It is our faith, a gift from Him. It is our reasonable expectation to believe and receive.

Expect to receive a return as you invest in the righteousness of Christ.

6 One Penny

The ballroom was impressive as was the welcome pack that they had received at the registration for the conference. Mack wondered why he had resisted so long signing up with the program when it was so very first class. All he really wanted to do was make some decent money so he could give more to his fellowship and to his friends in the mission field. That was the turning point for him in joining the organization. They said it was full of Christians whose desire it was to give more money to God. It looked to Mack like the Lord was really prospering these believers.

Making his way over to his sponsor's table he was even more impressed by the level of wealth he was surrounded by. Carl flashed him a million dollar smile and pumped his hand enthusiastically when Mack reached the table. The dinner was superb and the band that followed was excellent. The keynote speaker was as funny as any professional stand up comedian he had ever heard. Even with all the laughs he had managed to emphasize all the positive steps you needed to take to be a success in the business. There was a constant buzz and stir of excitement in the air.

As he was leaving the hall Mack felt warm and close to those in Carl's team. He knew many of them professed to be Christians. In fact if he didn't know better he would have thought he was in a church service. Mack hazarded to ask Jeff why he became one of the team. Jeff said it was because he wanted to help people and to make a difference. Without much thought as to protocol he asked Jeff if he gave to the church or any missions organizations.

Jeff paused and said: "Well, I intend to once I pass the hundred thousand a year level. You know you have to get your self established first and take care of your own family needs before you can give to others." Mack was astonished by Jeff's response. Conducting a mini-survey proved to him that many of the others saw giving the same way as Jeff. It wasn't a priority. The problem was they all had higher and higher levels of achievement that they had to reach before they would give.

Standing outside the hotel entrance Mack reached into his pocket and took out the only cash he had. Not much in light of all the others but it was his. Rounding the corner of the street he found a homeless person. As he gave him the cash he realized that he could start fulfilling his dream now.

* * *

Are you like Mack? Do you have friends in missions that could use some support? Does your church need finances? What about the local charities? Do you wish you could do something for the poor but feel you don't have enough?

The kingdom of God operates on the principle of sowing and reaping. Your ability to harvest is directly correlated to the amount of seed you sow. If you sow little, you reap little. If you sow much, you reap much. If you don't sow at all, you reap nothing.

The kingdom of the world says to reap you need to **stow**. Put money away in pensions and investments. Hold on to it and let it grow. Keep it and bank it is the only way.

If you sow much, you reap much.

The kingdom of God says that the wisdom of the world leads to poverty. We are to store up wealth in heavenly bank accounts where our investments can't be touch either by rust or moths. The only way to do this is to give some of your money away. Over the last couple of decades this kingdom advice has proven true. Major investment institutions have gone belly up with many people losing huge chunks of their pension savings. No amount of complaining and petitioning has been able to restore it.

God isn't against us having some money saved. In Proverbs He says the wise man will save for his children's children. But He does tell us the key to having some money in our life is to give and to start with what little we have. In Luke 16 he tells us that he who is faithful with little will be faithful with much.

God isn't against us having some money saved.

If you are unable to give of what you have, no amount of increase will cause you to feel more confident to give. Giving is an action of faith. We give because we believe that the unseen kingdom of God and its riches are sufficient for all our needs. We may not have an abundance of money in the bank but we are still able to give in faith. If you give 100 out of 1000, you are building trust and faith in God's ability to sustain you on the remainder. If you haven't developed your faith in small amounts, you will never be able to give 10 000 out of 100 000.

The time to see your faith fulfilled is now. Start with what you have and be amazed at God's faithfulness to honour those who honour Him. In fact God says in Malachi that we can test Him in the whole area of giving. Bring the whole tithe into the storehouse and test me. It is a challenge that the Lord has put before you. How much more confident can we be, if He has said he will more than match our offerings?

7 The Devouring

Chris was lost in thought as he pulled onto the motorway. He had done this so often his reflexes and actions were on autopilot. The car increased in speed to merge with the oncoming traffic with a slight hesitation and jerkiness. Chris never noticed. His mind was occupied with the declining number of cases at the office. The firm had been doing so well and new clients had been added every month for a year. Recently the work had diminished little by little. Neither he nor his secretary had initially had time to notice. Only this morning had she pointed it out to him. It really didn't make sense.

His mood was gloomy like the weather outside. The car jerked once again only more noticeably this time. The irregularity of the motion caught Chris's attention. He quickly glanced at the gauges but noted nothing unusual. It started to rain. How aggravating, he thought, just enough to make driving difficult and not enough to get the intermittent wipers to work right. Now I have to listen to that infernal squeaking.

His mind drifted back to the office as the traffic flow moved steadily. How could this have happened? He was one of the top young lawyers in the city. He was bright, enthusiastic and born again. God was on his side; who could be against him. This just didn't make sense.

Wonder how things are going at home? Hoping for some encouragement he called Julie.

"How's it going, Luv?"

"Horrid!"

Just what he needed to hear? "What do you mean: horrid?"

"Well," Julie sighed, "you wouldn't believe what happened today. The washing machine was full with a dark load and started into the full wash cycle, when bam it stopped. I couldn't get it to go. I couldn't get the door open. I finally drained the machine through a trap in the front panel at the bottom. Then I had water everywhere. What a mess! It is supposed to be on warranty but I can't find the card. The service company won't do anything without the code on the warranty. Where did you hide that?"

"I think", Chris began to say, when the car gave a series of lurches and began to loose power. Pointing for the shoulder lane of the highway Chris asked Julie to hold on a moment.

At the side of the road the car rattled and shook as if in a final death throe and gave up the ghost. "Julie, you won't believe this! The car just died on the motorway. Not only that the rain has really started to pelt down! I can't believe this. I'll talk to you later."

As he waited for the roadside assistance he prayed. "Lord, what on earth is happening? My life seems to be falling apart. This car is almost brand new and so is the washer. Why are the caseloads so low now? How will I pay the mortgage if this keeps up? Man, it seems like the enemy is having a heyday at my expense. I thought you said if I brought in the tithes and offerings you would rebuke the devourer for my sake." Wait a minute..... The tithe..... When was the last time I put it into the church? I had better call Julie.

"Jules, when was the last time we put in the tithe at church?"

"How would I know? You always take care of that. Don't tell me you haven't kept it up."

"Well, I don't know. You know I've been awfully busy at work. I thought you were keeping up the accounts."

"I have only been recording what I've been spending. But looking at our accounts right now it looks like nothing has been paid in three months."

"Ok, talk to you later."

"Well. Lord, you did say that he who honours you, you would honour. Sorry I haven't been doing that. I'll write a cheque when I get home and drop it in the post. Thank you for your grace and forgiveness."

* * *

Have you ever wondered what was happening to your life? Everything seems to break down and fall apart. You just seem to make some money and then unexpected bills come in that devour it. You never seem to get ahead. You work harder and harder only to pay more income tax with more bills and even more debts incurring. You still can't get ahead. In fact the thought of paying a tithe to God seems impossible. You are always short of money. How on earth are you going to pay 10 per cent more of it to God?

Have you ever wondered what was happening to your life?

Yet in Malachi 3: 8 - 12 God says through the prophet: "Will a man rob God? Yet you rob me. "But you ask, 'How do we rob you?' "In tithes and offerings. You are under a curse-- the whole nation of you-- because you are robbing me. Bring the whole tithe into the storehouse, that there may be food in my house. Test me in this," says the LORD Almighty, "and see if I will not throw open the floodgates of heaven and pour out so much blessing that you will not have room enough for it. I will prevent pests from devouring your crops, and the vines in your fields will not cast their fruit," says the LORD Almighty. "Then all the nations will call you blessed, for yours will be a delightful land," says the LORD Almighty." (NIV)

In this Old Testament book God clarified that the failure to bring the tithe into the storehouse had consequences on the fruitfulness of their labours. As Israel was an agrarian society He said He would rebuke the pests that were devouring the crops and prevent the vines from casting their fruit before they are ripe. In todays terms that would be protection over our wages and rebuking the errant bills that come up and seem to steal from us.

> *How it functions is under grace.*

God said that the people were robbing Him by not bringing in the tithes and offerings. Now DON'T immediately disregard this scripture as under the law and not grace! Let me explain how it functions under grace. In Malachi He was talking to people who knew what His will was but chose to ignore it. They understood Leviticus 27 and Deuteronomy 14, which gave instructions regarding the tithe under the law. They were not ignorant of the law. They were disobeying it.

The Lord said through the prophet, Samuel, to Saul, the king, in 1 Samuel 15:22: "Does the LORD delight in burnt offerings and sacrifices as much as in obeying the voice of the LORD? To obey is better than sacrifice, and to heed is better than the fat of rams." Although the Israelites had the law the Lord was looking for obedience to His VOICE. He essentially is saying to Saul I was looking for obedience rather than legalism. God is looking for the Spirit of the law not the letter of the law. The law was reflective of His will but not the complete expression of who He is. He spoke through prophecy and dreams to the people of God as well.

Jesus fulfilled the law. The word "fulfilled" means 1) to do what is necessary to bring about or achieve something expected, desired, or promised; 2) to do what is necessary to complete or bring something to an end and 3) to be good enough or of the type necessary to meet a standard or requirement. Jesus completed the requirements of the law. He did what was expected and necessary to bring to completion. Luke 24:44-45 says, "He said to them, "This is what I told you while I was still with you: Everything must be fulfilled that is written about me in the Law of Moses, the Prophets and the Psalms."

Then he opened their minds so they could understand the Scriptures." He not only fulfilled the requirements of the law but also that which was prophesied about the coming Messiah.

We who believe in Him and are baptized in identification with Him also then fulfill the law. It is done. The blood of Jesus wipes away all accusations and guilt. We have a clear conscience before God. Our sins are gone. We are new creations. We can go boldly into the throne room of grace to obtain mercy and grace in our time of need.

Having entered this freedom through the Spirit of the Lord we are being transformed in our soul.

No longer under the sentence of death and obligation we are free in Christ to follow His Holy Spirit. 2 Corinthians 3:17 - 4:2 says, "Now the Lord is the Spirit, and where the Spirit of the Lord is, there is freedom. And we, who with unveiled faces all reflect the Lord's glory, are being transformed into his likeness with ever-increasing glory, which comes from the Lord, who is the Spirit. Therefore, since through God's mercy we have this ministry, we do not lose heart. Rather, we have renounced secret and shameful ways; we do not use deception, nor do we distort the word of God. On the contrary, by setting forth the truth plainly we commend ourselves to every man's conscience in the sight of God." Having entered this freedom through the Spirit of the Lord we are being transformed in our soul. This is the essence of grace. We have the redemptive work of God providing us with not only salvation from death but also transformation into His likeness. This transformation is also the work of grace. Grace, which is the word "charis" in the Greek, is defined by Strong's Concordance as 'the merciful kindness by which God, exerting his holy influence upon souls, turns them to Christ, keeps, strengthens, increases them in Christian faith, knowledge, affection, and kindles them to the exercise of the Christian virtues.' Grace is the divine influence upon our hearts and its outward working. It comes from within not from without. Grace is not a one-time event but an ongoing influence in our lives. That influence comes

Grace is not a one-time event but an ongoing influence in our lives.

to us by the Holy Spirit. (Check John 16:5-16)

Remember Jesus asked his disciples in Matthew 16:13 - 17, 'Who do people say I am?' Simon Peter answered, "You are the Christ, the Son of the living God." Jesus replied, "Blessed are you, Simon son of Jonah, for this was not revealed to you by man, but by my Father in heaven." Peter did not get this truth through intellectual deduction but through revelation. The Spirit of God revealed the truth to Peter. We all come to the knowledge of Christ as our saviour and Lord by revelation. It is the work of the Holy Spirit in our lives. Equally the Spirit will teach and reveal the words of Jesus. When we have something revealed to us by the Holy Spirit, then we are to be obedient and walk in that truth. The letter of James says, "Anyone, then, who knows the good he ought to do and doesn't do it, sins." (James 4:17) The word of God is alive and active in our life. (Hebrews 4:12) The Spirit convicts us if we have sin or prompts us to walk this way or that.

In other words we are not to apply the law as the Jews did and obey it hoping for salvation. No one could meet the laws requirements except the Son of

God. Since he did, His Spirit comes to convict us to walk in the truth of God. This truth may be found in the Old and the New Testament for God gives us a progressive revelation of who He is. We need to be faithful to the revealed truth and walk in obedience to it.

For me that truth came to my wife and I as new believers. We kept feeling compelled to give and we had read about this word "tithe" in the bible but didn't understand what it all meant. We asked our friends who were leading our church what it meant and how to apply it. They explained it was Old Testament and we weren't under it. They gave a tenth from their net income and used it for things like flowers and gifts for people as well as giving to the church. But that didn't satisfy this quest for understanding that we were on. We then attended a weekend seminar with a preacher called Dennis Gibson. He taught on the Spirit led life including giving. He said that the government expects to take taxes off of our gross income so why would we expect God to take a tithe off of our net income. From that point forward we were convicted to tithe off of our gross income. We even tithed off of the excess money that was returned after our income tax was calculated. We didn't need to if we were following the Law of Moses as we had already tithed on that money. But we felt we were to bless the Lord with at least a tenth from any money that came into our possession.

A fellow challenged me many years later from our church about the tithe when we had been talking about giving. He asked me if I was free from the law or did I feel obligated to give the tenth. I told him that I wasn't under the Law of Moses but the law of the Spirit of life convicted me to give at least a tenth. (Romans 8:1-16) Bonnie and I had a revelation or conviction from God about giving a tenth to Him. It was not an external law that we were obeying but an internal work of grace upon our heart that convinced us, even compelled us, to give.

Have you ever had a revelation or a time that you knew the Holy Spirit was convicting you of something? Well, that is what we had regarding giving a tithe. It wasn't obeying the law but obeying the Spirit's conviction. When I withhold the tithe, the Lord gets my attention through means similar to those used in the illustration. We need to be faithful to the prompting of our conscience regarding the revelations the Lord has given to us. He will nudge us and nudge us to do what we know is the right thing to do. We don't have to because of the law. We do it because He has asked us and we know it pleases Him to respond willingly to His grace in our life.

All of this to say:

"It's a spirit led truth not an Old Testament law we are to respond to."

8 It's the Law

The offering basket passed down the row as the band played a worship chorus. The church had been in a period of teaching on money and stewardship, the significance of tithing and freewill offerings. Dan looked at the basket as it was handed to him. Once again he hardened his heart and let it pass.

He was not happy with all this teaching on finances. He was under grace and didn't have to give. All that tithing stuff was under the law. At least that's what his dad had taught him. He liked the church and the people, but he found the fact that they believed in tithing a real bother to him.

Later as he was leaving the church the pastor bumped into him. Dan was annoyed even though it was an accident. No longer could he contain his thoughts and much to the surprise of his pastor he blurted out: "Aren't we under grace and not the law?"

"What?" His pastor, surprised, replied.

"Aren't we under grace and don't have to tithe?" responded Dan. "My dad always taught me that tithing was Old Testament law and that we had been set free from the curse of the law. So why do you keep on and on with this teaching about tithing?"

Taking a deep breath the pastor regained his composure from this sudden outburst and attack. "Well, Dan, if you look carefully at the Old Testament, you will see that it is all about grace. Grace is God's favour given without reserve. He didn't just start doing that with the arrival of Jesus. He showed His favour to Abraham by calling him out and blessing him. But He didn't simply call Abraham to bless him alone. He called Abraham and his future generations to be a blessing to all mankind. They were to be emissaries of His kingdom to everyone. The book of Romans in the New Testament tells us that Abraham was righteous because he believed God not because he obeyed the law. God set up the whole system of sacrifice to deal with His people's sin so that He wouldn't have to punish them. He knew they couldn't fulfil the law so he said to them that they could sacrifice an innocent lamb whose blood would cover their sin. This was grace. They didn't get what they deserved. They knew His will and His law and still sinned. But He arranged for their sin to be covered. This is grace."

"Abraham operated under this grace before the law was given. He understood that it was because he believed God that he was justified. Even knowing that, Abraham, when he was greeted by Melchezidek the priest, the king of Salem, gave a tenth of all he had gained in plunder to Melchezidek. The New Testament book of Hebrews tells us that Jesus is a high priest in the order of Melchezidek. Melchezidek received the tithe as does Jesus."

"Many people think that Jesus abolished the law. He fulfilled it. He did what we could not do. Only through him can we fulfill the law. His blood shed for us covers us from our iniquities. He didn't abolish it, He satisfied it."

"But Jesus went a step further. He not only calls for our actions to be righteous but He calls us on our thoughts. What is in our heart is what defiles us. Our words often betray the condition of our heart. He has said that He loves a cheerful giver, one who does not give grudgingly or under any sense of compulsion. He is looking at the heart. Giving is a heart issue. Does He have your heart? Can He trust you to build his Kingdom? That's the issue"

"Dan, God has entrusted you with your income as a steward. You are responsible with what you do with it. If you can't give freely, trusting God to provide, then don't give. But don't stay there. Ask God to help you understand your role in giving. Paul in the second letter to the Corinthians says that we are to excel in this grace - the grace of giving."

"What's in your heart that stops you from giving - that's the issue?"

* * *

Many people are confused over the issue of giving as it relates to the law. They somehow feel that under the covenant of the New Testament they are exempt from any responsibility. They have missed the purposes of God for them. We upon receiving Christ become part of the family. We are restored to relationship with the Lord through the gift of life that Christ has given us. It is unearned but still has responsibility with it. The Lord's original directive was for Adam to steward the earth, to bring it under the rule and reign of the kingdom of God. Adam was His son and His representative upon the earth. Everything was given to Adam including the responsibility to tend the earth. God was willing to enter an interdependent relationship with man: a relationship where they worked together as partners.

The Lord has not changed His original intent for the earth. The sons of God are to reveal the kingdom of God to the earth. In the midst of the corruption and sin there is to be a witness to the redemptive power of the kingdom of God to all mankind. This is the plan. We take an active participatory part in the redemption of mankind. God has yoked himself to us in this work. The last chapter of Mark says that the apostles went everywhere preaching the word and the Lord confirmed it with signs and wonders.

We are the body of Christ, His expression on the earth.

Our life is hidden in His life. We are the body of Christ, His expression on the earth. He laid down His life for us so that we could live. Now we are to lay down our lives for Him so that others can live. Our life is to no longer be wrapped up in self-indulgence and selfish ambition. We are to be an example to others. We are to be a reflection of the goodness and mercy of Christ to others.

Part of this partnership is giving. We can give lip service to the preaching of the gospel. We can act like we are for the kingdom of God. But our commitment is spelled M - O - N - E - Y. It is a true indicator that we have embraced the mission and purposes of God for our life.

9 Famine

Not able to sleep Mark slipped out of bed and crept softly into the lounge. The last bill that came in the post that day gave him a nagging headache. As Mark prayed he was stymied and frustrated by the constant shortfall in the family's finances. For months they were short by at least 500. Their fellowship had taught that the way to deal with your financial problems was to give. Prosperity was God's desire for all His children. God would give you the desires of your heart. If you desired a big house with a pool, He would give it to you. Giving was the key to reaping.

As he prayed he reviewed his situation. He had been diligent in the tithe. He had given offerings. He had seen much fruit from his offerings. But for the last while something was different. Something was wrong.

What was it, Lord?

He waited. As he did so he began to realize how rarely he had listened for the Lord's voice in the last while. He hadn't bothered as he had everything pegged. All had been well and when the financial crunch had come he chose the way he had been taught. He contemplated how he had made a truth into a formula for maneuvering God to do what he wanted.

Asking the Lord to forgive him, Mark again chose to wait and listen. As he did he felt that inner voice speak to him. What he heard surprised him.

The Lord quickened to him an ugly incident he had had with an individual in the church. As he meditated on the whole affair he came to understand that although things seemed fine in outward appearances he had a definite lack of forgiveness in his heart towards them. In fact unconsciously he had been avoiding the other person for months, choosing to go the other way or ignoring phone messages. When he did talk to them, it was brief and to the point. No dillydallying.

'What do I do, Lord?' he prayed. The inner stirring was simple. Forgive them. As he prayed he forgave and asked the Lord to forgive him for holding this offence. He also sensed that he should drop them a note asking their forgiveness.

As he sealed the envelope he felt a sense of cleansing and renewed closeness to the Lord. Faith, hope and joy started to bubble within him as he crept back into bed. Today will be a great day was his thought as sleep closed about him.

* * *

It is human nature to look for formulas and methods to solve problems. Even in relationship to the Lord there is a tendency to look for package deals that make life work right. We can affirm with our mouths that Christianity is all about relationships and yet still fall victim to formulas, especially if they seem to bring success and prosperity.

One author wrote that our point of need is our point of fellowship with the Lord. His supposition is that our need will provoke us to fellowship with the Lord. Regardless of whether you agree or not, a need or a withholding of blessing is often the method used by the Lord to get our attention. He really is interested in a personal relationship with us, one that supersedes formulas and keys to success.

It is human nature to look for formulas and methods to solve problems.

Proverbs 30:7-9 says: "O God, I beg two favours from you before I die: First, help me never to tell a lie. Second, give me neither poverty nor riches! Give me just enough to satisfy my needs! For if I grow rich, I may become content without God. And if I am too poor, I may steal and thus insult God's holy name." (TLB) The author of this statement has recognised a reality to human nature. When things are going well, we become content and less attentive to the Lord. When need hits us, we will go to our knees in a heartbeat.

Look at King David in 2 Samuel 21:

The wheels created a dust eddy as the chariot sped along the road. The fields lay before the King parched and arid. What little growth survived was straggly and wispy. The spring harvest was indeed poor.

" Sheva, what is the report for the rest of the country?"

" Not good, my Lord. The stewards report that the entire country once again is devastated by drought."

" We need to head back to the palace. Surely we will be forced to increase our imports once again. How many years does this make it now?"

" Three years, King David."

" I must enquire of the Lord as to why this has come upon us. This is not a natural phenomenon. The Lord is obviously trying to get my attention."

At the palace David went before the Lord in prayer waiting to hear from Him as to the cause of these three years of drought. The Lord told David that it was because of the sin of Saul in violating the covenant with the Gibeonites that this had befallen Israel.

* * *

This event is an immense comfort to me. If David, who was a man after God's own heart, could take three years to hear the voice of God, I can relax when I don't catch on so quickly. Often people pass off one or two occurrences or happenings without much thought by simply assuming it is the common course of things. The third time is usually the clincher, the attention getter. Where you finally ask, 'Why is this happening?'

I have a tendency to flow along without much thought of the Lord when things are going well. I have great intentions of maintaining a close and intimate relationship with Him. Sometimes I have managed to do this but sometimes I slip up. Usually this happens when everything is going well. Like David or Mark we can miss the closeness of fellowship with the Father. When this happens, He uses a variety of means to catch our attention. One of the most effective is the lack of personal finances.

Is He punishing us for ignoring Him? Or, is He trying to get our attention? Could it be that He has been calling and calling gently to us and we have ignored Him? Could it be that He is more concerned with who we are and what we will be then we realize?

The New Testament says in Philippians that He is

at work in us to will and to do of his good pleasure. That it is the kindness of God that leads us to repentance. What is repentance? What is the Lord looking for in repentance?

Repentance is a change of heart. The heart speaks of the inner life of a person where their values, beliefs, opinions and attitudes are held. Jesus told us that out of the heart the mouth speaks. Our words are merely a reflection of our thoughts. The only way to change a heart is to allow the Holy Spirit to work in our life. This is the action of grace released in our life. Grace may, in one way, be described as the work of the Holy Spirit upon our heart and its outward working.

Repentance is a change of heart.

If we are working from a gospel that espouses simple formulas such as give to get, we may encounter some mystifying results. We may rebuke the Devil for all we are worth, only to find no change in our situation. The lack of change could damage our faith, as the formula didn't work. We actually find ourselves fighting against God who has no intentions of giving up until our lives are changed.

The Lord will in His mercy conform us to the image of His son. If we are not listening, He will use a lack of finances to catch our attention. He does desire to fellowship and to lead and guide us. Repentance is the pathway to increased intimacy and wholeness.

Grace is the work of the Holy Spirit upon our heart and its outward working.

10 Money, Money, Money

Tom's specialty lumberyard did not have a large number of customers to be cared for at any one time. This allowed Tom to engage each customer in conversation, which could lead to many interesting topics. Today a young man had turned the topic to spiritual ideas. They had talked about a variety of faiths and ideals while they were loading the cedar planks into the back of his pickup truck.

Tom asked if he had ever thought about the

teachings of Jesus.

"I think Jesus was a good man, but those guys on TV are something else. All they do is ask for money and then flaunt it with expensive clothes and jewelry. Jesus wasn't rich. He was poor. He wouldn't do that if he were here today," said Eric as he threw another 2x4 onto the bed of the pickup truck.

"So, you're convinced that Jesus was poor?" asked Tom.

"Yeah, that's what I've been told", replied Eric, "What do you think?"

"Well, the bible does quote him as saying he didn't have a place to lay his head unlike the birds or foxes. But it does say that Judas who betrayed him was his treasurer. You don't have a treasurer if you don't have any treasure do you? In fact when Judas left to betray Jesus to the Jewish leaders, the other disciples thought he was going to give money to the poor," said Tom.

"He had a treasurer!" exclaimed Eric.

"That's what the bible says. You know they must have had a lot of money because the bible also says Judas used to rob from their common purse. With a guy like Simon Peter around, Judas wouldn't have stood a chance getting away with it if they only had a little bit. Peter would have been all over it wanting to know where the money went."

"I didn't know that", said Eric. "But Jesus didn't have expensive clothes and fancy things, did he?"

Tom thought for a moment before he said, "Well, at the crucifixion the soldiers divided his clothes among them. But because his undergarment was seamless, woven in one piece from top to bottom, they threw lots for it. You don't gamble on a piece of cheap junk, do you?"

"Well, that's shakes up my ideas about Christ", said Eric. "Definitely food for thought!"

* * *

What is your perspective on wealth and God? Do you think like Eric that to be truly holy or blessed you need to be poor? Or do you think that the Lord might truly want to bless you?

What is your perspective on wealth and God?

The scripture, 'for the love of money is a root of all kinds of evil[1]', is often referred to as the reason why we shouldn't gain any wealth. The context for this scripture is about false teachers and their desire to use godliness for financial gain. Paul continues the statement above with "Some people, eager for money, have wandered from the faith and pierced themselves with many griefs[2]." The issue is not money - the issue is the love of it. Jesus said: "No one can serve two masters. Either he will hate the one and love the other, or he will be devoted to the one and despise the other. You cannot serve both God and Money[3]". We have to clearly choose which one we will serve.

---

1 I Timothy 6:10(a)
2 I Timothy 6:10
3 Matthew 6:24

Assuming you and I have chosen God as the one we love and will serve, we have to ask ourselves what is God's perspective regarding wealth and blessing His children. In the initial calling of Abram (Abraham) in Genesis 12:2,3 God said: "I will make you into a great nation and I will bless you; I will make your name great, and you will be a blessing. I will bless those who bless you, and whoever curses you I will curse; and all peoples on earth will be blessed through you." This blessing was tangible and evident to the people who lived near Abraham. He did receive Isaac, the child of promise, by faith when it was physically impossible for Sarah and Abraham to conceive the child naturally. But he also prospered financially as did Isaac and Jacob.

Under the Lord's direction Isaac planted during a famine and he reaped a hundredfold return because the Lord blessed him. Genesis 26 says: "The man became rich, and his wealth continued to grow until he became very wealthy. He had so many flocks and herds and servants that the Philistines envied him.[4]" The bible says he became rich, which by definition is wealthy.

[4] Genesis 26:13,14

In Deuteronomy 8, one of the books of the law, the Lord tells them that they are going into the Promised Land, which is flowing with blessings. He says to the people: "You may say to yourself, "My power and the strength of my hands have produced this wealth for me." But remember the LORD your God, for it is ***he who gives you the ability to produce wealth***, and so confirms his covenant, which he swore to your forefathers, as it is today.[5]" The Lord says just before these verses that He took them into the desert "to humble and to test you so that in the end it might go well with you[6]." Often we go through times of testing to see what's in our heart. Paul said in Philippians 4:11,12: " I am not saying this because I am in need, for I have learned to be content whatever the circumstances. I know what it is to be in need, and I know what it is to have plenty. I have learned the secret of being content in any and every situation, whether well fed or hungry, whether living in plenty or in want." What is that secret? In verse 13 Paul says he can do all things through Christ who strengthens him. It is putting Christ first in all situations. If your motive for serving God is financial gain, a time of need will certainly reveal your heart's desires.

---

[5] Deuteronomy 8:17,18 (Italics are mine)
[6] Deuteronomy 8:16

Although we may go through desert times of testing so that we will know what is in our heart, ultimately the result is the Lord gives the ability to produce wealth and blessing. Paul wrote to the Corinthians that they should excel in the grace of giving[7]. In chapter 9 of 2 Corinthians Paul says: "You will be made rich in every way so that you can be generous on every occasion, and through us your generosity will result in thanksgiving to God.[8]" These two chapters, 8 and 9, of 2 Corinthians talk about the heart attitude of generosity, which is a result of this wonderful grace He has poured out on us. Even in tough times we can be generous because He is our provision and source.

> *The Lord desires to bless you.*

Wealth is a ticklish issue with Christians. Somehow there is a feeling of guilt when believers talk about money. Some believers tell me that it is wrong to make money yet continue to pursue careers and financial advancement. That is similar to the argument that it isn't God's will to heal but still going to a doctor when you aren't feeling well. If we really

[7] 2 Corinthians 8:7
[8] 2 Corinthians 9:11

believe that healing is against God's will, then we are obviously in sin by seeing a doctor or going to the hospital. If we believe gaining wealth is against God's will, then pursing a better job for more money is wrong. Getting an education to improve your earning capacity is wrong. If poverty or lack is God's will for his children's lives, then we are fighting against His will every time we pursue employment.

Do a study of wealth yourself. I think you will see all through the Old Testament the Lord blessed his people financially. Look at the amount of money David gave towards the building of the temple. Try converting these amounts into today's valuations. There is often a table at the back of most bibles that gives you the ounce conversions of the differing weights. You can convert to ounces and multiple by today's gold and silver values. If God would do this for those under the Old Testament, how much more will He pour out upon those under the New Testament?

Jesus said: "Which of you, if his son asks for bread, will give him a stone? Or if he asks for a fish, will give him a snake? If you, then, though you are evil, know how to give good gifts to your children, how much more will your Father in heaven give good gifts to those who ask him![9]" How much more! We cannot out give God! He also said: "And do not set your heart on what you will eat or drink; do not worry about it. For the pagan world runs after all such things, and your Father knows that you need them. But seek his kingdom, and these things will be given to you as well.[10]"

The Lord desires to bless you. Place your faith in Him and don't restrict Him. Remember how often Jesus said to someone 'your faith has made you well'. Our faith pleases God according to Hebrews 11. Our faith frees or limits what He can do for and through us. Take the limits off God!

---

[9] Matthew 7:9 - 11
[10] Luke 12: 29 - 31

11 Faith for Giving

Sarah was struggling with the whole concept of tithing. As she looked around the meeting it appeared to her that no one else seemed to have a problem. Did they all really tithe? She knew tithing was the truth, that's why she was having such a problem. How could she possibly give away one tenth of her income when she always had too much month for her money? How did this work? The net income maybe she could swing. Never the gross! The government already takes so much off. How could she possibly give ten per cent of the total and still live? She felt overwhelmed.

The message had droned on in the background as she wrestled with her thoughts. Turning her attention back to the speaker she heard the words: "What's impossible for man is possible for God." The speaker had her attention now for as far as Sarah was concerned for her to tithe was impossible.

The speaker continued her message on how only God could do the impossible. She pointed out that the few references in the four gospels to the word "impossible" were to do with Mary having a baby as a virgin, Elizabeth conceiving in her old age, the idea that a man could save himself, and the resistance of demons to deliverance. All of these things are impossible with man. Unless............unless we have faith.

Only faith can move mountains. All of us face mountains - those obstacles that stand in opposition to God's will in our life. To see His will come to pass we need to move in faith. To see His heart for our world come to pass we need faith. Faith overcomes the world for it pleases God and He responds to our faith.

Sarah was lost once again in her own thoughts. This whole issue of tithing is impossible for me to do because I'm trying to figure out how I can do it. I can't. I have to move in faith and trust God that He will do the impossible when I obey His word to me. It's like salvation. I know I am saved because I believe, not because I see. Now I get it!

* * *

The ability to tithe and to give offerings above and beyond the 10% operates in the realm of faith. If you try to figure out how it works or how you are going to budget the money, you won't do it. Your "common sense" will tell you this is impossible, ridiculous and wasteful. It will tell you that no prudent person would do this, particularly on your income. Common sense will acknowledge that maybe someone with wealth could do this but not you. You already have more 'need' than income. Don't be silly.

Now common sense has it's place in life but it is not the final guide in what we do. Common sense often finds itself in direct opposition to the will of God and a life of faith. If we test the voice of God only against common sense, we will never do anything supernatural. Jesus said we would do what He did and more, but only if we move in faith.

Faith is what the just live by. Faith is the evidence of things not seen, the substance of things hoped for. Faith is a gift from God to begin with. And it is the ability to bridge the supernatural into the natural. It is the incredible evidence of the unseen world. It speaks of trust in God and hope for the impossible where it is beyond the ability of man.

> *If we test the voice of God only against common sense, we will never do anything supernatural.*

Faith allows us to give 10% and more of our income away in the trust that God is able to do abundantly more than we think or ask. Faith creates a reflection to the natural world of our absolute belief in God. Our ability to move or not move in the realms of prayer, healing, miracles and giving reveals our level of faith. Are we firmly ensconced in our own ability, rationale and common sense or are we willing to step out in faith and believe God for the impossible?

> *How does giving work? By faith, not logic!*

As the lead pastor in church I always check to see if a person is tithing before I will consider promoting them to positions of authority within the church. If they aren't, I won't give them that position of authority. I have two reasons for tithing as a standard for leadership. One, it shows that they are committed to the work at hand. If they don't believe in the work enough to support it financially, why would anyone they are leading support it? Two, it indicated the level of faith they have. If they aren't tithing, how can they lead us on in other arenas of faith? They would operate out of self, not out of trust in God. A church is a faith organization that should operates solely on trust in God. If we are to fulfill the vision God has given us, we have to be a people of faith. How could I possibly entrust leadership to someone who has not entrusted themselves to God at the level of faith for tithing?

How does giving work? By faith, not logic! God takes our offering and does the impossible for us. He honours the tithe and causes us to prosper. If He made the world out of what is not seen, how simple it is for Him to provide for us out of His abundance. Giving, tithes and offerings function out of faith. If we took the step to believe Him for salvation in Christ Jesus we can take the step and believe Him in our giving.

12 Paralysis of Fear

A conference on the Father's Heart of God was not where Pete wanted to be on the weekend, especially as it was for men only. The snoring and other obnoxious noises would keep him awake all night for sure. If it weren't for the fact that he was the pastor and had encouraged John to organize the thing, he would have stayed home. What could he surely gain from this? He had been a Christian for over twenty years. He knew God loved him.

The talk had not been entirely inspiring. Maybe it's just my attitude because everyone else seems to be enjoying the message. Now what? Oh don't tell me we are going to get touchy feely now. Brother, the break into small groups and pray thing! I would rather be at home watching the big game on TV.

Reluctantly Pete moved his chair into a circle to accommodate a group of three other fellows. I better get my act together seeing as I am the pastor. What was it Alex, the speaker, had asked us to do? Right, pray and see if God wanted to deal with any of us on the heart level.

As they closed their eyes in prayer Pete's thoughts drifted back to his childhood home. He remembered a long forgotten incident when he was about twelve. It was the first time he realized how often his dad wasn't home and that they didn't have any food. He was hungry, really hungry. His mother was simply standing looking at the empty table in the dining room. When he asked where dad was, she shed a tear for the first time that he had noticed and said she had no idea. When do we eat was his next question. She had apologized to him because there was nothing to eat. He had gone to bed that night very hungry. And as he thought about it he remembered that it wasn't the only time in his teens that it happened. His dad wasn't there and he didn't give his mother enough to keep them in groceries.

Pete shook his head. What a weird thing to come to mind. He didn't understand why he would think of that. Maybe he should share it and see if the other guys got any insight into it.

"I know this may seem a bit odd but as we were praying this incident is what came to mind. Maybe you can get some insight into this." And he related his thoughts to the other fellows.

John asked him if he struggled with the Lord's provision for him.

Pete was a little surprised at the question but said he did. He often felt like a beggar at a rich man's table and even though he tithed he struggled with the thought that there may never be enough. Although the Lord had never failed him, he did have nagging doubts and sometimes arguments within himself over whether he should tithe or not. He always did but he often struggled with it. This also made him feel badly as he knew the scripture said God loves a cheerful giver.

"So, what's this got to do with my mum and the hunger when I was twelve?"

"Well, we are at a conference on the Father's love for us. Alex was talking to us about how our perception of our earthly father as we are growing up affects our attitude to our heavenly Father. Your dad wasn't there for you in times of need, in fact, he seemed to create the situation for you. It's likely you developed distrust for his ability, or better yet, his willingness to provide for you. Now as an adult you are struggling to give joyfully and freely because you are wondering at the bottom of your heart whether your Heavenly Father will honour His word and bless you. I think you are struggling with fear of a lack of provision."

"I think you've hit the mark. I have had endless debates with myself over giving and being more generous because I know God's word. But, man, at points I have struggled and withheld. Then, I feel so condemned since I can't walk freely in what I know. The temptation is to not give at all. And it sometimes is horrible waiting for His provision to appear. Then I feel badly about that. It's a vicious circle that keeps harassing me."

"The key, I think," said John, "is to pray and forgive your father for his lack of provision and willingness. Then, ask the Lord to forgive you for holding this against your father. Then we'll pray and ask God to release faith in place of fear in your heart."

* * *

The intellect of a person can grasp the truth and yet they can struggle in the application of it in their life. This is due to the fact that more than our mind alone governs us. The Hebrews called the hidden seat of our emotions the heart. Jesus said it's what comes out of the heart that defiles us, not what we eat. Our words can sometimes reveal what is deeply seeded in us. Our actions will contradict what we profess as true too. We may want to do something and yet never get around to it because deep-rooted fears paralyze us.

Our words can sometimes reveal what is deeply seeded in us.

We may recognise these fears and try to overcome them by facing them and pressing through. We may accomplish the thing fear was holding us from doing but fear is always there - crouching at the doorway of our heart waiting until the next opportunity to undermine us. You find yourself once again facing a paralyzing attitude that you have to press through. You may even be mystified as to why this is so, feeling that you have conquered this fear before.

The problem with fear is that it is like a dandelion with a huge taproot deep down into our heart. We can pluck what we see off time and time and time again but unless we get the root, it comes back. The root may be a lack of forgiveness over situations that caused you pain or fear. It may be vows or judgments where you determined that you will never be like your father or mother or do what your parents did.

When we received Christ, we were forgiven all our sin. From that point on the Holy Spirit will convict of us of sin in our life so we can turn to Christ and receive forgiveness. At our new birth He cleanses us and then continues to cleanse us as we walk in a fallen world where we still have the capacity to get dirty. If we continue after we are born again to harbour an attitude of resentment and bitterness to someone, it will have an affect on the quality of our life. Remember Jesus came to give us life and that more abundantly. The good news is that He will not let us stay in a state of not forgiving that robs us of life. The Holy Spirit will continue to work in us to bring us freedom and life.

Often people create a theology that is rooted in fear.

Some people struggle in the whole area of giving because there is a deep-rooted fear that God really doesn't love them enough to bless them. Their earthly father never did, so why would this heavenly Father bless them. Their intellect may be well informed as to the truth of God and yet they struggle to walk in it. Often people create a theology that justifies their disobedience, which is rooted in fear rather than face the judgments they made many years ago that give the enemy a foothold to bind up their lives. We should ask the Holy Spirit to have His way in us by showing us those times and places where we judged another. It is only through repentance and forgiveness that we can truly be set free. Like Pete in the story the starting point for freedom is to recognise where we have bound ourselves through judgment. When you recognise you have made a judgment against another, then ask God to forgive you for judging them. Forgive the person you made the judgment against too as there's usually a reason for judging them. Then pray for a release in your finances or any other area the Holy Spirit shows you. You will walk in a new freedom and faith as a result of this prayer.

13 Enough to Give

The church service was like nothing David had ever been in before. There was so much joy and such freedom of expression. People sang, clapped and danced. The music was lead by a band of accomplished musicians. The worship went on for half an hour.

He was feeling a little intimidated by the whole thing, especially as his friend insisted they sit in the second row from the front. He had never waved his arms in the air before and wondered if everyone could tell.

The leader was encouraging them to give their tithes and offerings as part of their worship to God. David looked around for ushers or someone to pass an offering plate down the row. No one appeared. The band had started to play a worship song and all the congregation were joining in singing. Funny, he thought, that no one collected it.

He then noticed that people started to come to the front of the auditorium of their own accord. 'What on earth were they doing?' he thought. Watching them intently he saw that they were coming to wicker baskets set on stools at the foot of the staging. They were putting cheques, cash and envelopes with money, he assumed, into the buckets. Amazing!

David was quite taken with the whole process. Because the worship leader said visitors did not need to give, he had decided not to. But he could not take his eyes off the whole process.

'There's a sharply dressed fellow. Wow, look at the cash he gave! I'm impressed. Look at her, casually understated. She must be old wealth, nothing ostentatious about her. Man, I caught sight of the amount on that cheque. Whoa!'

'What am I doing snooping on these people? I had better pray. Forgive me Lord for being so curious. It is amazing though. Look at what they gave. You must be really happy. Even though he was impressed by the first two people he wasn't sure the Lord was as duly impressed. Something inside him told him that it was good but not as great as he thought.

He noticed what appeared to him to be a street person who came forward. He threw in a few coins and left. David's immediate thought was: big deal, lot of good that will do. As that thought passed through his mind a pain of immediate conviction struck him. 'What, Lord?'

In his spirit he felt the words of his Lord. "Why are you so impressed with the first two and not the last one? They gave out of their abundance that which they won't ever miss. He gave all that he had."

* * *

There is a thought in the western world that affects even Christian thinking. It is the idea that if we give, we give only out of what we will not miss. We have to have abundance first before we will consider it. Who would give out of their poverty? That's crazy. It's too costly.

Me first, the kingdom of God second!

The church in the west has often embraced the same thinking. Me first, the kingdom of God second! It shows up in gospel preaching that says salvation doesn't cost you anything. It's all there for you for free. Yet careful scrutiny of the scriptures shows us that God expects us to surrender our life to have his life in us. That is costly. It means we will go where he wants us to go, do what He wants us to do, and to love our lives not unto death. We overcome the devil by the blood of the lamb (that is what He did for us), the testimony of our mouths and that we laid down our lives even unto death (that is our part for Him)[11]. It is costly. Jesus admonishes us to count the cost or we will be like the man who starts to build a tower but doesn't have enough money to complete it.[12]

To think that there is no cost in following Christ is a travesty. How can we truly be His disciples if we are not prepared to lay down our life for Him? How can we say we are His disciples if we are only willing to give to His cause out of our abundance? Paul commended the Macedonians because they gave to the believers who were suffering in Jerusalem. The commendation came because they gave out of their great joy and their deep poverty.[13]

> *Poverty is not so much the lack of financial resources as it is a state of your mind*

[11] Rev. 12:11

[12] Luke 14:28

[13] 2 Cor. 8:1-4

Christ is looking for a people who will walk in obedience. Disciples are those who hear and do what their teacher says and does. Jesus gave tithes and offerings. Remember when Judas left the last supper to betray Him the others thought he was going to give alms to the poor.[14] He is not asking us to do anything that He has not done first. He knows the temptations we face to not be obedient. He understands and identifies with our cares and concerns. He will help us through any situation if we put our faith and trust in Him.

Can you give out of your poverty? Most certainly - when we respond in faith. Often people want to give but feel that they do not have enough income to possibly spare a tenth of it. They think it would be easier if they were making huge amounts. It isn't. For poverty is not so much the lack of financial resources as it is a state of your mind.[15] You could have bank accounts busting with money and still be fearful and afraid to give. There are accounts of people who lived like paupers but upon their death their estate was in

---

[14] John 13:29

[15] Matt. 26:11

the millions. The ability to enjoy money is a gift from God according to Ecclesiastes[16]. The amount you have does not determine whether you are truly wealthy. Whether you control it or it controls you determines if you are rich or still a pauper. Poverty is located in your heart not your hands.

Poverty is located in your heart not your hands.

[16] Ecc. 3:9

14 Answers

"So what's this tithing thing?"

"I don't know. It's something to do with giving. Have you been thinking about giving?"

"Yeah. All I know is that since I gave my life to Jesus I have been thinking more and more about giving. I was listening to a recording where the preacher mentioned tithing. And I know it's in the bible because I read about Abraham giving a tithe in that book section called Hebrews. So what do we do?"

* * *

Hopefully you have been thinking a great deal about giving. The encouragement to give is one thing, but how do you actually do it is another. How do you shift from one lifestyle to another? Let's answer the questions that you may have.

What's this tithe thing?

The tithe is a Hebrew word meaning a tenth. The Lord told His people to give a tithe of all that they earned. The tithe went to the Levites who then gave a tithe of that to the priests. The Levites were the Lord's inheritance and as such did not have a portion of land given to them like the other tribes. The tithe was to be their portion as His provision for them. So the tithe was a way of funding the men who acted as priests unto the Lord.

It is still an applicable principle for today. Paul encourages the church to consider those elders who preach and teach among them to be worthy of double honour. Double honour was double the income of others. The Lord calls men and women today to serve Him full time and the tithe is to be there to support them. Many church planters start off as bi-vocational, working a full time job while working full time as a pioneer in establishing a church. As the church flourishes the responsibilities increase to the point where they must devote themselves wholly to ministry. Finances need to be there to pay them. This is the point of the tithe. To spend the money on a church building is really wrong. Structures to worship the Lord in the Old Testament were built from offerings not tithes. Tithes support people who ministered to the Lord and to the people. We partake in spreading the gospel by helping to finance the people that God has given to the church to lead and equip it to do the work of service. The church needs leaders and leaders need support.

Are we to give a tithe of our income then?

It's a good place to start. Some people think that

it is under the Old Testament Law of Moses. Since Christ came and set us free from the curse of the law they say we don't need to tithe. The interesting thing about the Old Testament is the reference to three tithes, which the Jews still refer to as the First tithe, the Second tithe and the Poor tithe[17]. The people who think that the requirement was only ten per cent miss it by quite a bit. The deal with the Old Testament law is it showed the people what should be in their heart. But you can't legislate righteousness. The heart has to be changed. It wasn't until Christ came, died and was resurrected that it was possible to change the heart of a person. I don't know why people would think that if God thought that somewhere between ten and thirty per cent was sufficient under the old testament that He would change His mind and make it nothing under the New Testament - the testament that deals with our heart attitudes.

Do we give it on our take home pay or on our gross salary?

[17] International Standard Bible Encyclopaedia, Electronic Database Copyright (C) 1996 by Biblesoft

If the government gets their share off the gross, don't you think God should get His off the gross too? In the bible He always asked them to give Him the offering from the first fruits. The point is if you give, you'll get more. If you give to God first, you'll get more blessing. If you sow to the government first, what would you likely get back from them? More taxes. Do you want more taxes, then put them first.

How do you survive on what's left?

That's where faith comes in. If you honour God with the tithe, He will make sure the remaining ninety per cent goes further than the whole. Remember that faith is the substance of things hoped for, the evidence of things not seen. It is amazing what happens but you have to try it to see. That's why He says in Malachi to test Him in this and see what He will do.[18]

Who do you give it to?

[18] Malachi 3:10

Malachi says to bring the tithes and the offerings into the storehouse. A storehouse is local in that you can draw out of it. In the spirit where do you draw from? Who do you go to when you want prayer? Where do you go on Sundays? Who is your cell group associated with?

The church.

There's the answer. The church is real people touching real people. If your church is doing that, then that's the place to bless. You can give offerings to other ministries and people but honour the church you are involved with.

It is important for you to understand that the church is people - not just an organization. God uses the comparison of sheep and a shepherd for a description of His church. Both of them are interdependent on each other. Interdependent means that both parties could exist independently of each other but they chose rather to work together. The shepherd could live without his flock and the flock could possibly survive without the shepherd to care for them. But by working together the shepherd leads them to food, water and shelter. The flock follows, produces wool and meat both of which the shepherd can use to sustain himself.

The analogy that compares people in a fellowship to a flock of sheep is not very complimentary. But there is a strong reality in that the sheep are far less able to sustain themselves than the shepherd. Any church or organization that has lost its leadership will suffer. The evidence is all around us. If you are observant, you will have noticed that churches or organizations that have a sudden upheaval in leadership for whatever reason will always lose people. Where do these people go? Do they align themselves with another group right away?

When churches of 200 people split, you end up with two churches of 50 each or less. What happens to the other 100 people? They wander, as the scriptures say, like sheep without a shepherd. When the people of God neglected the tithe, the Levites went to other work than ministering to the Lord. They found other means to support their families. Who suffered? The nation. The spiritual climate suffers when there is a lack of godly leaders. When a church fails to supply the leadership support through tithes and offerings, the leader or leaders may suffer for a time but they will eventually find employment. But what happens to the church? Does it grow and prosper? Are people well fed spiritually? Are they winning the lost? The spiritual climate suffers.

Maybe a lay leader will take up the baton and give the group direction and impetus for a season. As it grows again it will require this leader to give more and more attention to the work and without support this is not possible. The growth will plateau and the size of the fellowship will eventually decrease, as the lay leader will not be able to sustain both.

When we are involved with a church, the leadership are there to teach, equip, guide and pray for us. They watch over us as a shepherd does his flock. Equally, the shepherd is cared for by the flock, which are providing for his/her needs. When we support our fellowship with tithes, we are supporting our leaders who are caring for us.

For the sake of the leadership of any church please find one where you respect the leaders and the vision for the fellowship. If you do, then show your support by giving. If you don't agree with them, do yourself and the church a favour by finding a new one where you are in agreement. God is a God of diversity. He has not created all fellowships the same. Find the one that you fit and then give of your time, energy and money. Amos 3:3 states: "How can two walk together unless they agree."

Because leaders are people, who are saved by grace like you and I, they can do things that offend us or upset us. If this happens we need to work the problems out through the understanding that we are in this together. But if you disagree with whom they are or where they are going, don't hinder the work but find a group you can support.

How do you tithe when your bills are more than you can now manage?

Firstly pray for God to give you grace and the Spirit's help. Giving is a spiritual exercise. Pray for

His wisdom and His help to implement giving in your life. Then put some planning into effect. This is very important. You might need to get some help working out a budget. Maybe you'll have to get a loan to consolidate your debts so that you have lower monthly payments and can tithe. It's important that you use some wisdom in the beginning so that you can honour your obligations and God too. If you need help, talk to your leaders and ask for some help.

Remember it is a step of faith. Faith works in the unseen and feels risky and uncomfortable. But it isn't faith if we can do it ourselves. Faith really trusts in the heart of God and His goodness to prove His love for us.

15 The Gift of Giving

"Hi Suzie! How are you today?"

"Great, pastor! I'm so happy to be at church this morning."

"Excellent! Love to hear that. How's your Dad?"

"He's really well."

"You know I've never seen or met your father. Does he go to church somewhere?"

"No, not anymore. He used to."

"What stopped him from coming? Is he a believer?"

"Oh yes, he's definitely a believer! He said he doesn't like to come to church because others in the church constantly ask him for a loan, as they know where we live and assume we have lots of money. He just feels almost pestered so he doesn't come."

"Wow! That's really unfortunate."

* * *

The heart of God is to give, to bless and to encourage all people. John 3:16 that is often seen as a placard being waved before cameras at major sporting events says, "For God so loved the world that he gave his one and only Son, that whoever believes in him shall not perish but have eternal life." The scripture says "whoever". That is open to everyone who believes, not just a select few with the right pedigree or social standing. It's available to everyone.

The Lord also says, "But I say to you, Love your enemies and pray for those who persecute you, so that you may be sons of your Father who is in heaven. **For he makes his sun rise on the evil and on the good, and sends rain on the just and on the unjust.**" (Matt. 5:44-45) Jesus is calling us to manifest the same character as His Father who not only blesses the righteous but the unrighteous too. He shows His love to all people in hope of them responding to His goodness and love. Love wins! He loves so that we will love.

His love extends to us in gifts that He showers upon us in abundance. In Ephesians chapter 4 beginning with verse 11 and 12 it says, "So Christ himself gave the apostles, the prophets, the evangelists, the pastors and teachers, to equip his people for works of service, so that the body of Christ may be built up". These people are a gift to the church, His Body. In Romans 12 scriptures says, "We have different gifts, according to the grace given to each of us. If your gift is prophesying, then prophesy in accordance with your faith; if it is serving, then serve; if it is teaching, then teach; if it is to encourage, then give encouragement; if it is giving, then give generously; if it is to lead, do it diligently; if it is to show mercy, do it cheerfully". These seven gifts are sometimes called motivational gifts or gifts from the Father. They are to help us express the love of the Father to people around us. In 1 Corinthians 12 there are the gifts of the Holy Spirit. "Now to each one the manifestation of the Spirit is given for the common good. To one there is given through the Spirit a message of wisdom, to another a message of knowledge by means of the same Spirit, to another faith by the same Spirit, to another gifts of healing by that one Spirit, to another miraculous powers, to another prophecy, to another distinguishing between spirits, to another speaking in different kinds of tongues, and to still another the interpretation of tongues. All these are the work of one and the same Spirit, and he distributes them to each one, just as he determines." We are told in verse 7 that theses gifts are given for the common good. In 1 Corinthians 14 it says that prophesy is given for the purpose of our strengthening, encouraging and comfort.

In Deuteronomy chapter 8, as has been mentioned before in this book, God tells us that 'it is he who gives you the ability to produce wealth'. This is a gift. As stated above in Romans 12 according to The Passion Translation the word says, "*If you have the grace-gift of giving to meet the needs of others, then may you prosper in your generosity without any fanfare.*" This translation calls it the 'grace-gift'. Paul refers to this in 2 Corinthians 8 where he says, "But since you excel in everything—in faith, in speech, in knowledge, in complete earnestness and in the love we have kindled in you—see that you also excel in this grace of giving." Paul explains that giving is a grace we can excel at, as we can with faith and love. In Strong's concordance grace is defined as the divine influence upon the heart and it's outward working. Grace, unlike the law, works on and through our heart, which only God truly knows. This grace transforms us to be like our Heavenly Father and our Saviour Jesus. Like all the gifts there is an enablement

...see that you also excel in this grace of giving

of the Holy Spirit that empowers us to flow in the gift of giving. At the beginning of chapter 8 Paul says, "And now, brothers and sisters, we want you to know about the grace that God has given the Macedonian churches. In the midst of a very severe trial, their overflowing joy and their extreme poverty welled up in rich generosity. For I testify that they gave as much as they were able, and even beyond their ability". Do you see that their giving came out of the grace that God had given them? They actually gave during very difficult circumstances described as extreme poverty. Yet they did it with overflowing joy. This is the grace of God working within and out of their hearts.

Now Paul is calling every believer to give without exception. 2 Corinthians 8 in verse 12 says, "For if the willingness is there, the gift is acceptable according to what one has, not according to what one does not have". It isn't about the amount of the gift nor the proportion of income as much as it is about the willingness to give. Our attitude is key to our giving, so much so that Paul goes on to say in chapter 9 that He is looking for cheerful givers, not those giving out of compulsion or

Our attitude is key to our giving

grudgingly. If we give willingly we will see increase coming to us. We may not have the 'gift of giving' flowing through us but that does not excuse us from giving. Paul expects us to all respond as a result of the grace of God in our life.

We, as believers, can function to some extent in the different activities of the Spirit. We can prophesy, teach, serve, encourage, lead and give. We may not have the gift of a teacher or a prophet or of one gifted to give but it is not to stop us from responding to the prompting of the Holy Spirit. But when you have a gift, you will find there is an enablement to do whatever it is. It is easy. I have a relative who is gifted as an evangelist. He flows in it so easily that I am envious (remember we can covet the gifts according to 1 Corinthians 12:31 KJV). I have imitated what he has said to people while watching a sporting event. He said to a group of parents that he was flying to the Philippines the next day. They asked him why and he explained about going to preach the gospel to the people there. I tried it at a parent school event when I was flying to the Philippines to minister. For him the people responded with great interest, for me they said, 'oh' and turned away. The difference is the gift. The gift opens doors as it says in Proverbs.

(I'm not talking of a bribe but the outworking of the gift of God).

When it comes to the gift of giving, money is accessible. Many believers who are wealthy have this gift, but it isn't limited to them. My father in-law had this gift. He worked for the railway and the union on a set salary. He also gave beyond twenty per cent of his income. At one time in Canada the government accepted twenty per cent of charitable giving as a deduction from your taxes. My father in-law always had monies above and beyond that amount which he could carry forward to the next year. He never could use that money, as the next year would again find him giving more that the twenty per cent. He continued to do this with his fixed pension. God would bless him in many ways. So much so that my other relatives thought he was obviously a millionaire. If you have this gift and you don't withhold, money comes to you. You're like a money magnet.

The condition of our heart is the central issue in our life of giving. Jesus had an encounter with a rich man in Mark 10 who wanted to know how to inherit eternal life. "Jesus looked at him and loved him. "One thing you lack," he said. "Go, sell everything you have and give to the poor, and you will have treasure in heaven. Then come, follow me." At this the man's face fell. He went away sad, because he had great wealth." (Verses 21, 22) Jesus had commended him on his following of the law but saw that there was one thing he lacked – that was the ability to give to the poor.

The gift in and of itself has a sense of reward and blessing. Sharing it particularly when it is money can be difficult. For once people realize you have the funds and the freedom to give they will come seeking what you have. Jesus experienced that. In John 6 He was sought out by the crowd whom the day before he had fed miraculously from five small loaves and two small fish. He said to them in verse 26, "Very truly I tell you, you are looking for me, not because you saw the signs I performed but because you ate the loaves and had your fill". Our stomachs dictate much of what we seek. I had a friend who gave a testimony of a wonderful physical healing and how the Lord had blessed him with $10,000 in the same week. He told me after the service people only approached him wanting to know more about how the money came. No one was interested in the supernatural healing, which he thought was the more significant of the two events.

In Luke 17 ten men who had leprosy appealed to Jesus to cleanse them of this disease. He told them to go show themselves to the priests to verify their cleansing. As they went they were cleansed. One realizing he was cleansed returned to praise and thank Jesus. In verse 17 and 18 Jesus' response was, "Were not all ten cleansed? Where are the other nine? Has no one returned to give praise to God except this foreigner?" When you minister in the gifting God has given you, often people receive it and go on their way without any thought to you or your part in what they received. As a believer you have to return again and again to who is my source? The approval of man will fall far short if you are looking for it.

Like the prodigal son found when his inheritance was gone so were his party buddies. Once the gift is gone, so are the seekers. This is difficult with any gift you have from the Lord. People respond because they heard you have an anointing for healing or teaching or prophesying or caring. After they have what they desire they are off about their own business.

One fellow I know who was a very effective prayer counsellor and able to set people free from demonic bondage told me that the people whom he spent hours with in the process of seeking freedom often totally ignored he and his wife at Christian events. They acted as if they didn't know them or even saw them. It didn't stop him from ministering to others but it did hurt to be spurned.

> *Our heart is precious and needs to be protected as well as open and forgiving.*

Many whom I know that have the gift of giving have encountered the plea of one person after another who need a loan that they promise they will pay back. Most of the time they never see a penny of it return to them. Like the man in our vignette one has to be wary of hardening one's heart to the people whom God has given you a gift to minister to. To say you will never give to anyone again, or not go to church because someone might approach you for funding, is like a teacher saying I will never teach the word again as all the people ever do is take, take, take and then don't apply it. Or the person with a gift of healing saying I'm never going to pray for the sick again as all they want is my gift and never thank me for it. Our heart is precious and needs to be protected as well as open and forgiving.

Each gift requires a level of sensibility and responsibility. James says in his letter to the churches, "not many of you should become teachers, my fellow believers, because you know that we who teach will be judged more strictly". When I first started to lead a church as a pastor, I found it particularly frustrating at how accountable the Lord kept me in my lifestyle compared to others in my congregation. I felt my leash was so short and others seemed to have so much leniency extended to them by the Lord. I was whining to Him one day in my prayer time about how unfair this was when He spoke correction to me. He spoke into my spirit that the particular person I was complaining about was His little lamb and He treated her with that in mind. But I was His shepherd and He treated me with this in mind. He said that He required much more from His shepherd who was responsible for His flock then He did from the lambs. Then He directed me to the scripture in James' letter. What could I say? I repented for driving His lambs instead of gently loving and leading them.

In fact Jesus said in Luke 12 that to whom much is given much is required. The Passion Translation says, "For those who have received a greater revelation from their master are required a greater obedience. And those who have been entrusted with great responsibility will be held more responsible to their master." This scripture is spoken in the context of Jesus' interpretation of His parable of the faithful steward waiting for his master's return from a wedding banquet. He tells Peter that someone who knows very little will be corrected less severely than the person who knew what the master asked and yet didn't do it.

> *All the gifts require nurture, preparation and discernment*

My point is: our gifts are our responsibility. We need to be faithful in the fulfilment of them within our community.

All the gifts require nurture, preparation and discernment. One needs to nurture the gifts God has given us. One line from a children's song that stuck years ago in my mind was "practice makes perfect". A gift will come to you so naturally that you may not even realize how gifted you are. Because it is easy you think everyone can do it. But they can't. Even so, the best athletes, musicians, performers and preachers strive to be better, to excel in their gifting. They do not take it for granted. They also connect with others that have the same gift. We went to a meeting of a well-known prayer ministry in London one evening. When we left, my wife was teary-eyed but so refreshed from the time spent there. On the way home she said to me that those are my kind of people, meaning the same gifting, which stimulated her gift.

Before I move in my teaching gift, I give time to personal reading of the Lord's word. I pray, communing with Him and I praise Him. My wife and I share our revelations of what He is doing in our lives as part of the nurturing. Then I pray about what to teach. If it is a subject I have taught many times, I still seek the Lord for fresh revelation. I make note of scriptures that I feel impressed to use, which results in a fairly intense bible study. Then I pray for more clarity and finality as to what I am to say to His people. I also have to discern the age of the group I'm addressing, the situation in the church, how well I know them and they know me. As I'm preaching I'm also listening to the Holy Spirit for more inspiration, any changes I should make, whether the people are understanding my message, whether they are with me or if I've lost them.

So it is with those who have the gift of giving. Your personal relationship with the Lord is crucial. You are one of His sheep so you will hear and recognize His voice. With the number of requests you will receive you need to know if you should give, how much you should give or if it's unwise to give to this cause, person or church. It takes a keen ear to the Spirit and sharp discernment. One couple I know who have substantial funds, at one time did not give their whole tithe to their local church, as they knew it would damage the church. The maturity of the church is important in terms of how much funding they receive. Also it is important for a church not to lean on one person's financial giving. I know of one church that had a major giver who sustained the ministry. They had a staff of 14 or so, but when the giver moved, they had to cut back significantly the positions they had. One group in a foreign country had a fellow who was very effective in leading people to the Lord as he worked with them in the rice paddies. He would then start a church; call the organization of which he was a member to send a pastor from their bible school and he would move onto another region, starting again. The organization did not have huge financial support but decided they wanted to bless him with $5.00 (US) a month. He ended up no longer working at anything but sat at home waiting for this monthly stipend. One of their leaders said to me that who would have thought so little money could ruin so effective a minister.

Discernment and timing is key to this gift. One year my wife and I believed we heard the Lord direct us to enrol our two youngest children in a Christian school. We felt He said He would provide the funds for us to do this for them. On the basis of what we felt He had said, we enrolled them and expected funds would come from somewhere. The first month there was nothing extra coming into our household funds. This went on for six months of the school year. We paid the fees, while severely cutting back on other activities and expenses. It was a very lean six months. At the end of the six months a friend had dinner with us where he presented us with a cheque that covered

Discernment and timing is key to this gift

the entire year's fees. He said he knew he was supposed to do this for us in September at the beginning of the school year but he also felt the Lord say, 'Wait until I tell you to release the funds'. He said the Lord told me now is the time so here are the funds to pay for it. Believe me we were very grateful to receive that cheque.

Why did it take so long? Maybe as we have often found He wanted us to act on what we heard by faith to show our obedience. The word "provision" could be seen as 'pro' meaning 'for' the vision. Often His provision follows our action towards the vision. We believed God spoke, we acted on it, we continued despite financial adversity because of our faith in what He said and we were rewarded. Some people do not act on the word of God to them because they are waiting for the money to appear before they do it. God generally says 'go' and I will be with you. In Mark 16 the disciples went everywhere preaching the word and the Lord followed confirming it with signs and wonders. They preached

> *Ultimately we all, no matter what our gifting is, need to see God as our source.*

first and He validated it. I have often wanted Him to act first and then I could validate it.

For those with the gift of giving you have an awesome responsibility to rightly handle your funds. You need ears to hear what the Spirit is saying. Is it "yes", "no", or "maybe but not now". Ultimately we all, no matter what our gifting is, need to see God as our source. Not man, not some investment scheme, not some talent that could be monetized, but God. We need to repent if we are looking to man instead of Him. We all have that responsibility.

My prayer for you with this gift is: "May your heart be soft and gentle, may you forgive those who have despitefully used you and your resources, may you bless as the Holy Spirit directs you and may you prosper in all you set your hands too".

16 Accusation

The warmth of the sun's rays falling on Jim's face caused him to awaken with a sense of joy and well being that it was going to be a great day. Not a cloud in sight! Happily shuffling into the bathroom to splash some water on his face Jim felt a bolt of fear strike his stomach. He wanted to double over with the impact yet realized that it was not physical. As he stared into the mirror thoughts of hopelessness and fear clouded his mind.

Where was the money going to come from next? What would he do when the renters moved out? What was going to happen to them? Would they have enough?

All the joy of the morning was gone. A cloud of gloom hung over him as he showered and dressed. He felt abandoned and, worse yet, helpless. What could he do? There was no way that he could increase his income in his present situation.

As he headed down the stairs to the kitchen he thought of how ridiculous this was. Why was he so afraid? They had thousands in the bank account that would last them for quite awhile. Why was he so downhearted over something that wouldn't affect them for at least two months? Why was he so concerned that God wouldn't supply for his family and him after all these years of providing all that they needed? Why did he feel like it was all up to him, all his responsibility, after all these years? Why would the question of leaving ministry and what God had called him to do, suddenly be so real an issue in light of this future uncertainty? The last twenty years of his life had been one of faith and following the will of God for his life. How could he wake up on such a beautiful day and suddenly feel that he would be left financially ruined?

On top of the fear came a level of condemnation that made the whole thing worse. What kind of Christian is he, that he would doubt God's provision for his life? How could you so quickly think of leaving ministry? How could you only think of yourself and your family's needs? What about all those people who work with you in the ministry? What a hypocrite! If they could only see how fearful you are, they wouldn't follow you and your great vision!

At last Jim started to pray. The thought came to him that his wife and a team of people where ministering in another community that weekend. What have they stirred up? Wake up, man! This is the enemy; this is spiritual warfare. This is totally irrational in the light of the facts. This is fear and it is demonic in origin. It has no basis and it does not glorify God. Wake up! Pray.

As he prayed the gloom began to lift. His declarations of the goodness of the Lord brought a lightness and joy. His reviewing of the past faithfulness and provision of the Lord rekindled his faith. The despair and hopelessness started to pass. His joy returned as he sang songs of praise to the Lord.

The trial passed and peace returned. Jim was left with one question. How does this happen?

* * *

Have you ever experienced what Jim did? Have you ever asked yourself why this can happen? Have you ever thought that there must be something fundamentally wrong with your faith that this can happen after all these years? Have you thought that you had dealt with all your natural father issues that you used to project onto your heavenly Father?

The bottom line is that we all, every member of the human race, have an enemy who wants nothing more than to steal everything from you, kill you if he could, and destroy all that remains. This enemy hates you so much that he would be like the person that who, if he hit you with his car, would stop and run back over you numerous times to destroy any remnant of you he could.

> *When he looks at you, whether you realize it or not, he sees your heavenly Father.*

Why? Because he is consumed with hatred for the one who created you in His image. When he looks at you, whether you realize it or not, he sees your heavenly Father. You may be in total rebellion to your heavenly Father but that does not erase the fact that you are a reflection of his image. My oldest son looks very much like me. Genetics have predetermined that he will reflect my image to people who know us both. He can go places and meet people who immediately identify him with me. It might not make him happy but there is nothing he can do about it. Those who like me will probably respond favourably to him. Those who don't like me aren't going to be open to him. Sure he's a different person but it is the image of me that people recognise.

It is important to understand this simple fact: you have an enemy. It gives explanation to what Jim and others go through on their walk of faith. Adam and Eve encountered his wiliness in the Garden of Eden in Genesis chapter three. In his encounter with Eve he accused God of withholding from them. He implied that God didn't love them enough to trust them with everything. He accused God of withholding something that was good and desirous to have. After she had eaten and Adam too, they acquired the knowledge of good and evil which left them aware of their nakedness and vulnerability. They had never felt that before. They became fearful. When God came to talk and relate to them, they hid. When God called out to them, Adam answered that "I heard you in the garden, and I was afraid because I was naked; so I hid." (Gen. 3:10) What was his response upon hearing God's approach? Fear!

Since that time the enemy has manipulated this vulnerability (this propensity to fear) in man to drive him away from God and in turn, to accuse God for all the misfortune that has happened to him. Adam never stepped up to the bat and took responsibility for what they did. He blamed Eve and in the same breath blamed God.

Fear still affects us today. The enemy uses it to bring us into false positions of vulnerability where we end up accusing God instead of praising Him. We accuse Him of putting us in this position where we have nothing, where we feel vulnerable, insecure, and exposed. The enemy suggests that God doesn't love us; that He is withholding from us. The enemy's power over us is fear.

The word tells us that Jesus was like us in everyway except He didn't sin. Philippians chapter two and verse six to eight says that Jesus, did not consider equality with God something to be grasped, but made himself nothing, taking the very nature of a servant, being made in human likeness, and being found in appearance as a man, he humbled himself and became obedient to death – even death on a cross. Having done so, Hebrews chapter four says that we do not have a high priest (Jesus) who is unable to sympathize with our weaknesses, but we have one who has been tempted in every way, just as we are – yet was without sin. So He is in every way aware of the human experience.

Did he experience what Adam and Eve

experienced in the Garden? Did he experience the same doubts and fears that Jim experienced that morning?

Jesus is in every way aware of the human experience.

Of course he did. In Luke chapter three we have the account of his water baptism with John the Baptist. In verse 21 it says: "When all the people were being baptized, Jesus was baptized too. And as he was praying, heaven was opened and the Holy Spirit descended on him in bodily form like a dove. And a voice came form heaven: "You are my Son, whom I love; with you I am well pleased." At the beginning of his earthly ministry he has this wonderful affirmation of His Heavenly Father. He tells Jesus that He loves him and He is proud of him. What a blessing! To have your father tell you he loves you and that he is pleased with you is wonderful.

You know God would have told Adam that too. If you follow the genealogy through in Luke, you find that Adam is referred to as the son of God. Jesus is considered to be the last Adam because He did what the first son of God failed to do. He did not yield to temptation. Instead He took on the sins of mankind. He did not yield to fear neither did he blame God for the situation. He did not sin as Adam did.

Was he tested as Adam was? Luke chapter four says that he was tested by the devil three times while in the wilderness. He was alone as Adam was alone. No support group to encourage him to do the right thing. In two of the temptations the enemy accused his relationship with his Heavenly Father by saying if you are the Son of God. If God really loves you, you can do this and get away with it. The same proposition as he put to Eve. If you do this, you will be like God. She already was. We still are all made in His image. We still all reflect something of the nature and glory of God. But like Eve we are presented with the challenge: Does God really love you? And this challenge is always accompanied with fear. I'm vulnerable, exposed, naked....

> *What a blessing! To have your father tell you he loves you and that he is pleased with you is wonderful.*

The key to overcoming this is to recognise it for

what it is – an attack of our enemy. It is irrational, irreconcilable with whom our Father is. It feels very real, and will become so if you choose to receive it. Resist the temptation to give in. Fight! Confess the goodness of God in your life. Make a book of remembrance where you record all the times the Lord has provided for you. In some form or another record all the answered prayers, the healings, the jobs, the houses, the opportunities He has provided for you. When the enemy comes with the accusations and the fear, get your record out and remember what God has done for you. Then declare in faith what He will do for you now. Drawing into God is an action of humility, where you humble yourself before Him. Then, you can resist the devil and he will flee. The devil cannot resist someone who has gone into God. His victory is in having us pull away from God, to retreat and hide in fear.

If you want to live a life of victory in Christ, one of abundance, you need to understand that fear will coming knocking on your door. When you want to move out in faith, you will be challenged. When you feel prompted to give, you will face fear. Fear - that says you won't have enough - that says you are crazy - that God will never supply your needs - will come often, as you believe God and desire to move out in faith. Faith is not an absence of fear. Faith is trust in the word of God and acting upon it.

Because we know good and evil we know that there is a possibility of failure. We know that we are insufficient within ourselves and that we do not have the means to do what we feel called to do. We know what the good is we should do but fight to do it because of our self-preservation instinct that came with the knowledge of good and evil. Faith is a decision to obey in the face of fear.

Understand that fear will coming knocking on your door.

Most decisions to give will be challenged by fear. But giving is a true reflection of our heavenly Father's nature. To not give is a reflection of our old fallen nature, which we have so gloriously been set free from by accepting Jesus into our life. The choice is ours – to whom will you respond: your old self or your new man?

17 Where's My Heart In This Matter?

Where is my heart? This is the question we all have to ask ourselves. The answer to that will determine where we will invest our worldly wealth. If my heart is turned to the Lord, then we will give as disciples to the work of the kingdom. If it is turned to our own pleasure, security, fears and concerns, then we will give to those things all the attention that our heart can muster.

Over the years I have observed the outward actions of people. I am unable to judge the intents and motives of the heart but I am aware that out of the heart the mouth speaks. Their words have often been a disappointment when it comes to the area of giving. Their actions as exemplified by their offerings in the offering plates have been hugely discouraging.

I have taught, exhorted, possibly, even bullied people into giving into the work of the kingdom, with little resultant change in the offering. I have seen people refuse to change, refuse to give, and justify it by saying, 'God told me that it is ok not to.' I have seen others take the step in faith and enter the wonderful adventure of giving to God. I have heard their testimonies of the faithfulness of God to supply all their needs.

The common denominator seems to be the condition of the heart.

The common denominator seems to be the condition of the heart. This conclusion is reached only by observing the actions of people. The New Testament is clear that it is a heart issue. We are exhorted to give voluntarily without a sense of compulsion. We are to be willing, not grouchy, but cheerful when we do. If we are being strong-armed or giving under obligation, there won't be any expressions of joy.

Paul in Philippians 4:18-20 says: "I have received full payment and even more; I am amply supplied, now that I have received from Epaphroditus the gifts you sent. They are a fragrant offering, an acceptable sacrifice, pleasing to God. And my God will meet all your needs according to his glorious riches in Christ Jesus. To our God and Father be glory for ever and ever. Amen." (NIV) How can he say that gifts to him are acceptable sacrifices pleasing to God? They become a fragrant offering when Paul received them with thanksgiving and praise to God for the gifts. Paul did not require these of the Philippians as an obligation to fulfill his apostolic authority over their fellowship. This was a gift given under no obligation, no request or demand, but freely. He would have been filled with praise to God for their faithfulness and grace unto him. Hebrews 13 says that we give to God

> *The only thing we can give to Him directly is our praise.*

an offering that is the fruit of our lips: a sacrifice of praise. As one person is blessed by another there springs forth a gushing of praise for God's goodness. The only thing we can give to Him directly is our praise. Genuine praise comes out of the heart changed by a loving God.

Are you giving? Yes – good! No! Why not ask God if this is His will for your life? Don't let fear or common sense undermine your faith. If you are afraid, ask Him why? Be willing to deal with the reasons that hinder you. Remember poverty is a state of mind not finances. I have known wealthy people who were terrified to let any earthly possession go because of a fear of not having enough. Fear is not reasonable. It does not deal with the facts, but only distorts them. True freedom is being released to do whatever God asks of you.

If you are giving but feel no joy in it or are under a sense of obligation, then ask God to deal with the roots of the issue. We are to be fit vessels for the master's use. Ask the master what it is that is hindering you from living in the freedom and the abundance that Jesus promised. Allow Him to massage your heart through repentance. Don't resist Him, and don't ignore Him.

My hope for you as I close this book is that you will enter into the joy of serving your Lord in this wonderful grace of giving. It is a tremendous adventure that He calls us to. We need to be the ones that release the mooring lines to set sail on the sea of faith. Only you can make the decision to enter the realm of faith that will create a life that inspires others to write biographies about it.

Follow your heart and give.

18 Epilogue

The Lord prompted me to write this book several years ago. I thought it was a most unusual topic but after some debating with Him over the appeal and profitability of writing about giving I submitted to His wisdom and wrote.

These pages are an account of our discovery of His heart's desire to give and His desire that we follow in His footsteps. It is a compilation of our life story of passionately pursuing the Lord Jesus Christ with all our heart. Over the last 40+ years we have lived a life of giving.

Our experience validates that He is faithful and never fails to provide for His children. We have raised four children while living a life of faith. He has supplied all our needs and desires whilst living in Canada and England. We have travelled to over 30 countries for ministry and pleasure. There were times when we had a salary from an organization and other times when we had no fixed income. Regardless of the size of the salary or the absence of one He has provided all of our needs. There have been challenges, as His timing is definitely not bound to our sense of timing. But the joy of seeing God come through time after time has been wonderful.

Was it always easy to give? No! There were many times when I debated with Him over the sensibility of giving at that exact moment in our financial life. But the scripture, "To obey is better than sacrifice, and to heed is better than the fat of rams", from 1 Samuel 15 would come to mind. I often have thought this obedience is also a huge sacrifice.

One time I was doing our household bookkeeping. The bills far exceeded our resources and I was whining to the Lord about His lack of provision. He interrupted my monologue and told me to stop whining. Then I felt in my spirit that He said, 'Look at the books.' I said 'The Bible?' as He used the plural of books. He said, 'No, look at all the books that you use for your receipts and accounts'. I then said, 'These 3 ring books'. He said, 'Yes. I paid for every one of those bills. Why wouldn't I pay for these ones?' I stood corrected. He did provide for every one of the outstanding bills.

If you are longing for a life of adventure and opportunities to exercise your faith, then give to the works of God's Kingdom. You will find a life of excitement and fulfillment unlike any other. Jesus said, 'Seek first his kingdom and his righteousness, and all these things will be given to you as well'.[19] All these things are food, clothes, and homes - the things that the world is worried about acquiring. They will be yours too! Let the adventure begin!

[19] Matthew 6:33

ABOUT THE AUTHOR

Jim is a spiritual entrepreneur. He has asked the question "Why can't we?" throughout his Christian walk. Over and over the Lord has answered, "yes, you can." Jim has pastored churches, planted churches, started leadership colleges, co-pioneered a church movement, and developed marriage and parenting seminars with his lovely wife, Bonnie. Together they wrote 24 Secrets to Great Parenting.

Jim is an author and international speaker. He has a Father's heart and has four wonderful children of his own and a great many spiritual children.

His greatest passion is to teach others how to "do the stuff" of the Kingdom of God. 2 Timothy 2:2, "And the things you have heard me say in the presence of many witnesses entrust to reliable men who will also be qualified to teach others", has been his life's inspiration.

OTHER BOOKS AND RESOURCES BY JIM AND BONNIE INKSTER

24 Secrets To Great Parenting

(paperback)

Jim and Bonnie share from their vast experience the principles that helped them raise four great children. It is written in a light-hearted, easy reading style perfect for the busy parent with very little spare time on their hands.

Available through Amazon and on Kindle.

8 Questions Every Parent Wants Answered (DVD)

Jim and Bonnie surveyed hundreds of parents to find what issues are their greatest concern regarding their children. Eight questions were consistent from parents throughout the world.

These questions have been addressed in a powerful and entertaining format. Each session takes less than 10 minutes with great ideas for successful application within your family.

Available through Amazon

24 Secrets to Great Parenting

(audiobook)

Jim and Bonnie felt that this great book had to be available to everyone including those who don't like to read. The research shows men prefer to listen, women prefer to read.

Jim was professionally studio recorded reading this charming and helpful book. Great for in the car or on your personal player when exercising or simply chilling.

Eyes of Wonder

By Jim Inkster

(paperback)

Eyes of Wonder is a delightful collection of life experiences with the children and grandchildren that have taught Jim everything he needed to know to be an adult.

Similar to the Chicken Soup for the Soul series this gives you simple downhome wisdom. Always good for a chuckle too!

Available through Amazon and on Kindle

Under His Wings: Psalm 91: A Devotional

Bonnie Inkster

(Paperback)

Under His Wings is a devotional that powerfully extrapolates each verse into the fullness of meaning using references to other portions of scripture to illustrate all that it is meant to be. You can read a verse a day and ponder on all its goodness towards us the rest of the day. Equally you might want to read it all at once and then go back through it at your leisure. Either way the word of God is equivalent to a two-edged sword cutting a swathe through the enemy's lies and deception. The word is alive and active and as effective today as when it was first written. The word is discerning between the thoughts and intents of our heart bringing them out of hiding, exposing them to our understanding and allowing us to know who we truly are.

www.ingramcontent.com/pod-product-compliance
Lightning Source LLC
LaVergne TN
LVHW011329080426
835513LV00006B/252
* 9 7 8 1 9 9 9 4 2 5 1 0 4 *